That I may know God

That
I may know
God

pathways

to spiritual

formation

KENNETH BOA

Multnomah Publishers *Sisters, Oregon*

THAT I MAY KNOW GOD

published by Multnomah Publishers, Inc.

and in association with the literary agency of Wolgemuth & Associates, Inc.

© 1998 by Kenneth Boa
International Standard Book Number: 1-57673-281-9

Cover photograph by Photonica

Scripture quotations are from:
New American Standard Bible © 1960, 1977 1995 by the Lockman Foundation

Multnomah is a trademark of Multnomah Publishers, Inc. and is registered
in the U.S. Patent and Trademark Office. The colophon is
a trademark of Multnomah Publishers, Inc.

Printed in the United States of America

For information:
MULTNOMAH PUBLISHERS, INC.•POST OFFICE BOX 1720•SISTERS, OREGON 97759

Library of Congress Cataloging-in-Publication Data:
Boa, Kenneth.
    That I may know God/by Kenneth Boa.
        p.cm.
    ISBN 1-57673-281-9 (alk. paper)
    1. Spiritual life—Christianity. I. Title.
BV4501.2.B593   1998
248.4—dc21   98–18708
                                                            CIP

98 99 00 01 02 03 04 05 — 10 9 8 7 6 5 4 3 2 1

I dedicate this book with love to my father,
Kenneth Boa.

I have been blessed with a growing relationship with my dad,
and our weekly phone calls
are always a source of joy.

Contents

Preface

I was exposed to a number of strong Christian influences as I was growing up, but I didn't have a personal encounter with Jesus Christ until a month after graduating from Case Institute of Technology. That summer of 1967 was a strange one indeed as I moved to Berkeley, California. I was a new Christian still immersed in the fleeting "flower child" culture. During the next six months, I had virtually no contact with other believers, and I was in a painful transition. My mind had been filled with Darwinian evolution, the occult, and Eastern thought, but there was a gradually emerging Christian worldview. Six months after my conversion, I found myself at Dallas Theological Seminary. Dallas was a radical culture shock for me at that point in my journey! It took two semesters before the things I had previously learned finally began to converge in a coherent framework based on a growing understanding of Scripture.

In the years that followed, I was exposed to a wide variety of approaches to spiritual formation and discipleship. What has been particularly fascinating to me is how each of these approaches was presented with finality. Their proponents claimed that their style of spirituality was the best available. Each time I plunged in, I discovered another set of useful tools, but the toolbox never seemed to be complete.

At one point in my journey, I discovered the spiritual disciplines and immersed myself in them. At another point, I found myself captivated by writings that centered on the "exchanged life"—Christ's life for our life. There was yet another period during which I focused on the spiritual life as a product of being filled and empowered by the Spirit. I also went through a time when spiritual warfare became particularly real for me. The same thing happened with each of the other facets of spirituality, and I began to see a pattern. As important as each of these approaches has been to me, no one of them is sufficient; there is always more.

This has been a source of both frustration and excitement for me. Frustration, because my quests for a quick fix, a one-size-fits-all, or a controllable technique have all failed. Excitement, because I am beginning to see that we can hardly scratch the surface of all that God has for us, and that there are always new surprises. Seen this way, the pursuit of God becomes the greatest adventure of all.

In *That I May Know God* and its sequel, *Following Hard after God*, I want to present a more synthetic and comprehensive approach to the spiritual life. It will expose you to a number of beneficial approaches. Each of these has value as part of a greater whole. It is my hope that these books will stretch your thinking and encourage you to "press on toward the goal for the prize of the upward call of God in Christ Jesus" (Philippians 3:14).

I pray that as a result of reading *That I May Know God*, you will:

♦ develop a greater appreciation for the unique way God has made you,

♦ become aware of a wider array of options for your spiritual journey,

♦ get out of a possible spiritual rut,

♦ desire to experiment with other facets of the faith,

♦ appreciate the manifold legacy that has been bequeathed to us by those who have gone before,

♦ expand your horizons and be encouraged to move out of your comfort zone, and

♦ have instilled in you a greater passion for Christ and a greater desire to participate in His loving purposes for your life.

A Gem with Many Facets

These days, religion is out but spirituality is in. There has been a remarkable hunger and quest for spiritual answers to the big questions of life in the last three decades. In the past, there was a general moral consensus in the Western world that was loosely based on a Judeo-Christian worldview. However, this was accompanied by a growing tendency to secularize culture by marginalizing religion and replacing it with a popular faith in scientific progress and humanistic inquiry. But pure naturalism corrodes by the acids of its own assumptions. As the modern quest to arrive at final answers and solutions to the human condition by means of unaided human reason began to totter and crumble, the quest for transcendent solutions became more appealing.

In the postmodern world, there is a new skepticism about the quest for objective truth, a new relativism concerning moral standards, and a new multiculturalism that encourages us to pick and choose from a cafeteria of ideological options. This smorgasbord mentality of popular culture has led to a frightening lack of discernment and an uncritical openness to pantheistic spiritualities and New Age philosophies and techniques. In our time, one can freely promote Native American spirituality, Eastern mysticism, Western European paganism, shamanic medicine, techniques for achieving cosmic consciousness, or any form of yoga without fear of public criticism.

Taking their cue from education and the media, people are becoming more antagonistic to any authority that appears to be external or traditionally based. Thus, religion is on the way out while spiritualities that appeal to inner subjective and experiential authentication are on the way in. As the former Soviet Union shows, humans cannot live in an ideological vacuum; when one ideology is abandoned, people quickly embrace another, whether for weal or for woe.

Paralleling this growing popular interest in spirituality, there has been a pronounced increase in the church's appetite for spiritual renewal. The problem here is that many, especially certain leaders in mainline denominations, have failed to discern "the spirit of truth and the spirit of error" (1 John 4:6). Reimaging of God in radical feminist categories (e.g., the worship of Sophia and Gaia), Buddhist Tantrism, Hinduistic meditative techniques, and pagan symbolism have been surfacing more frequently in churches that have moved away from the authority of Scripture to espouse liberal theologies. Nevertheless, there are authentic, biblically orthodox, and time-tested approaches to the spiritual life that are taking hold in many communities of believers, and this is what this book means when it uses the term "spirituality."

From a human standpoint, there are a number of reasons for the growing awareness of spirituality among followers of Christ. Here are a few:

- ♦ the influence of the ambient cultural interest in spirituality
- ♦ growing dissatisfaction with the shallowness and sterility of the Christian subculture
- ♦ a more serious quest for meaning, purpose, and significance among followers of Christ
- ♦ greater availability and exposure to the classics of spirituality
- ♦ a more intense movement toward accountability and discipleship, and
- ♦ influential writers and teachers who have become committed to communicating about spiritual truths.

A JOURNEY AND A PILGRIMAGE

The concepts in this book describe a journey into spirituality. The spiritual life is an all-encompassing, lifelong response to God's gracious initiatives in the lives of those whose trust is centered in the person and work of Jesus Christ. Biblical spirituality is a Christ-centered orientation to every component of life through the mediating power of the indwelling Holy Spirit. It is a journey of the spirit that begins with the gift of forgiveness and life in Christ and progresses through faith and obedience. Since it is based on a present relationship, it is a journey *with* Christ rather than a journey *to* Christ. As long as we are on this earth we never arrive; the journey is not complete until the day of our resurrection when the Lord brings us into complete conformity with Him.

This journey with Jesus is really a spiritual pilgrimage in that we have confessed that we are "strangers and exiles on the earth" (Hebrews 11:13). Once we are in Christ, we become sojourners and aliens on this planet; our citizenship has been changed from earth to heaven (Philippians 3:20), and we must grow in the realization that no earthbound felicity can fully satisfy the deepest God-given longings of our hearts. During this brief pilgrimage, the terrain we encounter varies from grassy meadows to arid deserts and treacherous mountains. This pilgrim life is filled with joy and travail, with pleasures and afflictions, with clarity and confusion, with assurance and doubt, with comfort and pain, with relationships and alienation, with hope and despair, with obedience and disbelief, with confidence and uncertainty. But there are two critical truths to bear in mind when our surroundings become precarious: (1) others have preceded us in this journey, and some have left maps along the way to guide us through the territory ahead; and (2) God has equipped us with the spiritual resources He knows we will need throughout the journey.

TWELVE FACETS OF SPIRITUALITY

There are a variety of approaches to the spiritual life, but these are really facets of a larger gem that is greater than the sum of its parts. The diversity and complexity of the spiritual paths that have been taken by godly pilgrims of previous centuries is rich and impressive. These paths were blazed through courage and suffering and through reciprocity with complex historical, social, and cultural rhythms. Unfortunately, most followers of the Way have ignored the topographical maps that have been left behind or have torn off all the parts that are unfamiliar to them. The most common stumbling stone is to mistake a part for the whole. Like the blind men who feel different parts of an elephant, one assumes that the spiritual life is a trunk, another takes it to be a tail, and a third concludes that it is a leg.

Anyone who studies the four gospels should be suspicious of an approach that reduces the nuances of the spiritual life into a single formula or method. The gospels are not biographies, but highly selective thematic portraits that reveal different aspects of the life of Christ that should stand in dynamic tension with one another. The synergism of this tensioned interplay resists neat categorization, and so it is with the dynamics of a Spirit-led journey with Christ. In contrast to the conceit of those who seek to quantify and control, the humility of wisdom always whispers that there is more, much more. When we approach the spiritual journey with an open and teachable spirit, we will continue to gain fresh insights from the Word of God, the people we meet, and the books we digest.

That I May Know God and its sequel, *Following Hard after God*, take a broad and synthetic approach to spirituality by looking at several facets of this gem and seeing how each of them can contribute to the larger whole. I do not claim that the twelve facets presented in these books are exhaustive, but they do cover a substantial part of the terrain. While the discussion of each of these facets is fragmentary and sketchy, I have tried to distill the essence of each of these diverse but complementary approaches.

The following is a survey of the twelve facets that will be developed in *That I May Know God* and *Following Hard after God*:

1. *Relational Spirituality: Loving God Completely, Ourselves Correctly, and Others Compassionately*

As a communion of three Persons, God is a relational being. He is the originator of a personal relationship with us, and our high and holy calling is to respond to His loving initiatives. By loving God completely, we discover who and whose we are as we come to see ourselves as God sees us. In this way, we become secure enough to become other-centered rather than self-centered, and this enables us to become givers rather than grabbers.

2.   Paradigm Spirituality: Cultivating an Eternal versus a Temporal Perspective

This approach to spirituality centers on the radical contrasts between the temporal and eternal value systems and emphasizes the need for a paradigm shift from a cultural to a biblical way of seeing life. The experience of our mortality can help us transfer our hope from the seen to the unseen and realize the preciousness of present opportunities. Our presuppositions shape our perspective, our perspective shapes our priorities, and our priorities shape our practice.

3.   Disciplined Spirituality: Engaging in the Historical Disciplines

There has been a resurgence of interest in the classical disciplines of the spiritual life, and this approach stresses the benefits of these varied disciplines. At the same time, it recognizes the needed balance between radical *dependence* on God and personal *discipline* as an expression of obedience and application.

4.   Exchanged Life Spirituality: Grasping Our True Identity in Christ

The last century has seen the growth of an experiential approach to the spiritual life that is based on the believer's new identity in Christ. Identification with Christ in His crucifixion and resurrection (Romans 6; Galatians 2:20) means that our old life has been exchanged for the life of Christ. This approach to spirituality moves from a works to a grace orientation and from legalism to liberty because it centers on our acknowledgment that Christ's life is our life.

5. Motivated Spirituality: A Set of Biblical Incentives

People are motivated to satisfy their needs for security, significance, and fulfillment, but they turn to the wrong places to get their needs met. This approach emphasizes the option of looking to Christ rather than the world to meet our needs. A study of Scripture reveals a number of biblical motivators: these include fear, love and gratitude, rewards, identity, purpose and hope, and longing for God. Our task is to be more motivated by the things God declares to be important than by the things the world says are important.

6. Devotional Spirituality: Falling in Love with God

What are the keys to loving God, and how can we cultivate a growing intimacy with Him? This approach explores what it means to enjoy God and to trust in Him. We gradually become conformed to what we most love and admire, and we are most satisfied when we seek God's pleasure above our own.

7. Holistic Spirituality: Every Component of Life under the Lordship of Christ

There is a general tendency to treat Christianity as a component of life along with other components such as family, work, and finances. This compartmentalization fosters a dichotomy between the secular and the spiritual. The biblical alternative is to understand the implications of Christ's lordship over every aspect of life in such a way that even the most mundane components of life can become expressions of the life of Christ in us.

8. Process Spirituality: Being versus Doing; Process versus Product

In our culture, we increasingly tend to be human doings rather than human beings. The world tells us that what we achieve and accomplish determines who we are, but the Scriptures teach that who we are in Christ should be the basis for what we do. The dynamics of growth are inside-out rather than outside-in. This approach considers what it means to be faithful to the process of life rather than living from one product to the next. It also focuses on the expressions of abiding in Christ and practicing His presence.

9. Spirit-filled Spirituality: Walking in the Power of the Spirit
Although there are divergent views of spiritual gifts, charismatics and non-charismatics are in agreement that until recently, the role of the Holy Spirit has been somewhat neglected as a central dynamic of the spiritual life. This approach considers how to appropriate the love, wisdom, and power of the Spirit and stresses the biblical implications of the Holy Spirit as a personal presence rather than a mere force.

10. Warfare Spirituality: The World, the Flesh, and the Devil
Spiritual warfare is not optional for believers in Christ. Scripture clearly teaches and illustrates the realities of this warfare on the three battle fronts of the world, the flesh, and the devil. The worldly and demonic systems are external to the believer, but they entice and provide opportunities for the flesh, which is the capacity for sin within the believer. This approach develops a biblical strategy for dealing with each of these barriers to spiritual growth.

11. Nurturing Spirituality: A Lifestyle of Evangelism and Discipleship
The believer's highest call in ministry is to reproduce the life of Christ in others. Reproduction takes the form of *evangelism* for those who do not know Christ, and *edification* for those who do know Him. This approach regards evangelism and edification as a way of life; lifestyle evangelism and discipleship is the most effective and realistic approach to unbelievers and believers within our sphere of influence. In this way, ministry becomes an extension of being, but it cannot be measured. Evangelism and edification relate to our global and unique purposes in life.

12. Corporate Spirituality: Encouragement, Accountability, and Worship
We come to faith as individuals but we grow in community. A

meaningful context of encouragement, accountability, and worship is essential to spiritual maturity, since this involves the other-centered use of spiritual gifts for mutual edification. This approach stresses the need for humility and unity in the body of Christ as well as the importance of servant leadership.

A quick look at these twelve facets underscores how truly different we are from one another. As you read them, you were undoubtedly more attracted to some of these approaches than to others. You probably thought that some of them would be very hard for you, but easier for some of your friends to pursue. Some of them may be unfamiliar, and you may not have encountered people who have taught or practiced them.

As Paul puts it so beautifully in 1 Corinthians 12-14, the body of Christ is a diverse and composite unity in which the members exhibit different gifts and different ministries. It is good that we are different and that we need each other to grow into fully-functioning maturity, because no component in the body can be complete without the others.

It can be liberating to discover that because of our unique temperaments and circumstances, we are free not to be drawn to some approaches to spirituality. I suggest that before you proceed to the chapters that follow, this would be a good time to look at appendix A, "The Need for Diversity," where these differences are discussed in detail. As this appendix shows, some of us are extroverts and can never be alone, while others are consistently drawn to solitude. Some of us base our decisions on detailed investigation and others play it by ear and can move quickly, almost instinctively, through life. Some of our friends say we place too much of an emphasis on thinking and not enough on feeling, or vice versa. Our many temperamental differences are reflected in the way we practice the different facets of spirituality.

We shouldn't be ashamed of our differences. We can see how God has used dissimilar people throughout the history of the ancient, medieval, and modern church, and this is the focus of appendix B, "The Richness of Our Heritage." C. S. Lewis said that he preferred theological reading to devotional books, and great intellectuals from John Calvin to Thomas Aquinas have always been numbered among God's people. Martin Luther's approach was balanced by his friend and coworker Philipp Melanchthon. Francis of Assisi called the church to change in very different ways than John Chrysostom.

The appendix on the history of spirituality provides perspective and a sense of proportion concerning the ways in which God has used a great diversity of people through the centuries. It is because of this that we inherit a great legacy of different models and approaches from those who have gone before us.

Five of these models await us in this book.

——

Relational Spirituality

LOVING GOD COMPLETELY

WHAT IS MAN, THAT YOU TAKE THOUGHT OF HIM?

The God of the Bible is infinite, personal, and triune. As a communion of three Persons, one of God's purposes in creating us is to display the glory of His being and attributes to intelligent moral creatures who are capable of responding to His relational initiatives. In spite of human rebellion and sin against the person and character of the Lord, Christ bore the awesome price of our guilt and inaugurated "a new and living way" (Hebrews 10:20) by which the barrier to personal relationship with God has been overcome.

Our Greatness and Smallness

Human nature is a web of contradictions: we are at once the grandeur and degradation of the created order; we bear the image of God, but we are ensnared in trespasses and sins; we are capable of harnessing the forces of nature, but unable to rule our tongue; we are the most wonderful and creative beings on this planet, but the most violent, cruel, and contemptible of earth's inhabitants.

In his *Pensées,* Pascal described the dignity and puniness of humanity in these words: "Man is but a reed, the most feeble thing in nature; but he is a thinking reed. The entire universe need not arm itself to crush him. A vapour, a drop of water, suffices to kill him. But, if the universe were to crush him, man would still be more noble than that which killed him, because he knows that he dies and the advantage which the universe has over him; the universe knows nothing of this."

The Glory of God

Psalm 8 explores these twin themes, sandwiching them between expressions of the majesty of the Creator of all biological and spiritual life: "O Lord, our Lord, how majestic is Your name in all the earth" (vv. 1a, 9). The living God has displayed His splendor above the heavens, and He has ordained praise from the heavenly host to the mouth of infants and nursing babes (vv. 1b–2). When, after our Lord's triumphal entry into Jerusalem, the children cried out in the temple, "Hosanna to the Son of David," the chief priests and the scribes became indignant and Jesus quoted this passage to them (Matthew 21:15–16). Their simple confession of trusting love was enough to silence the scorn of His adversaries and "make the enemy and the revengeful cease" (v. 2b).

In verses 3–4, David's meditation passes from the testimony of children to the eloquence of the cosmos: "When I consider Your heavens, the work of Your fingers, the moon and the stars, which You have ordained; what is man, that You take thought of him? And the son of man that You care for him?" From the time David wrote those words until the invention of the telescope in the early seventeenth century, only a few thousand stars were visible to the unaided eye, and the universe appeared far less impressive than we now know it to be. Even until the second decade of our century, it was thought that the Milky Way galaxy was synonymous with the universe. Now this alone would be awesome in its scope, since our spiral galaxy contains over two hundred billion stars and extends to a diameter of 100,000 light-years (remember that a light-second is over 186,000 miles; the 93 million miles between the sun and the earth is eight light-minutes). But more recent developments in astronomy have revealed that our galaxy is a member of a local cluster of some twenty galaxies, and that this local cluster is but one member of a massive supercluster of thousands of galaxies. So many of these superclusters are known to exist that the number of galaxies is estimated at well over a hundred billion.

What is man, indeed! The God who created these stars and calls them all by name (Isaiah 40:26) is unimaginably awesome; His wisdom, beauty, power, and dominion are beyond human comprehension. And yet He has deigned to seek intimacy with the people on this puny planet and has given them great dignity and destiny: "Yet You have made him a little lower than God, and You crown him with glory and majesty!" (v. 5). While these words are applicable to all people, they find their ultimate fulfillment in Jesus Christ as the quotation of this passage in Hebrews 2:6–8 makes clear.

We were made to rule over the works of God's hands (Psalm 8:6–8), but we forfeited this dominion in the devastation of the fall ("but now we do not yet see all things subjected to him"; Hebrews 2:8b). But all things will be subjected under the feet of Christ when He returns (1 Corinthians 15:24–28), and we will live and reign with Him (Romans 5:17; 2 Timothy 2:12; Revelation 5:10; 20:6).

As wonderful as our dominion over nature will be, our true cause of rejoicing should be in the fact that, if we have placed our trust in Jesus Christ, our names are recorded in heaven (Luke 10:20). "What is man, that You take thought of him? And the son of man, that You care for him?" The infinite ruler of all creation really *does* take thought of us and cares for us, and He has proved it by the indescribable gift of His Son (2 Corinthians 9:15; 1 John 4:9–10). In the words of C. S. Lewis, glory means "good report with God, acceptance by God, response, acknowledgment, and welcome into the heart of things. The door on which we have been knocking all our lives will open at last." Let us exult in hope of the glory of God!

GOD'S LOVE FOR US: CAUSELESS, MEASURELESS, AND CEASELESS

We have seen that the love of God is the wellspring of biblical faith and hope. Consider these truths about the love of God from Paul's epistle to the Romans: In the book of *nature,* God reveals His

eternal power and divine nature (Romans 1:20), and in the book
of human *conscience,* He reveals our imperfection and guilt
(Romans 2:14–16). But it is only in the book of *Scripture* that
God reveals His limitless love that can overcome our guilt and
transform us into new creatures in Christ. God's loyal love for us
is causeless (Romans 5:6), measureless (Romans 5:7–8), and
ceaseless (Romans 5:9–11). There was nothing in us that merited
or evoked His love; indeed, Christ died for us when we were His
ungodly enemies. God's love is spontaneous and unending—He
loved us because He chose to love us, and having responded to
Christ's offer of forgiveness and relationship with Him, nothing
can separate us from that love or diminish it (Romans 8:35–39).
This means that we are secure in the Lord's unconditional love;
since we belong to Christ, *nothing we do can cause God to love us
more, and nothing we do can cause God to love us less.*

As people who have experienced pain and rejection caused by
performance-based acceptance and conditional love, the description
above seems too good to be true. Isn't there something we must do
to merit God's favor or earn His acceptance? If we are afraid others
would reject us if they knew what we are really like inside, what of
the holy and perfect Lord of all creation? The Elizabethan poet
George Herbert (1593–1633) captured this stinging sense of
unworthiness in his superb personification of the love of God:

> Love bade me welcome; yet my soul drew back,
>   Conscious of dust and sin.
> But quick-eyed Love, observing me grow slack
>   From my first entrance in,
> Drew nearer to me, sweetly questioning,
>   If I lacked anything.
> "A guest," I answered, "worthy to be here."
>   Love said, "You shall be he."
> "I, the unkind, ungrateful? Ah, my dear,
>   I cannot look on thee."
> Love took my hand, and smiling did reply,
>   "Who made the eyes but I?"

"Truth, Lord, but I have marred them; let my shame
    Go where it doth deserve."
"And know you not," says Love, "who bore the blame?"
    "My dear, then I will serve."
"You must sit down," says Love, "and taste my meat."
    So I did sit and eat.

Beyond all human faith, beyond all earthbound hope, the eternal God of love has reached down to us, and in the ultimate act of sacrifice, purchased us and made us His own.

How do we respond to such love? All too often, these revealed truths seem so remote and unreal that they do not grip our minds, emotions, and wills. We may sing about the love of God in worship services and learn about it in Bible classes but miss its radical implications for our lives. Spiritual truth eludes us when we limit it to the conceptual realm and fail to internalize it. We dilute it through cultural, emotional, and theological filters and reduce it to a mental construct that we affirm more out of orthodoxy than out of profound personal conviction. How do we move in the direction of loving God completely?

LOVING GOD COMPLETELY

In the last several years, I have adapted and used this prayer by St. Richard of Chichester (1197–1253) in my own quiet times before the Lord:

Thanks be to Thee, O Lord Jesus Christ, for all the benefits which Thou hast given us; for all the pains and insults which Thou hast borne for us. O most merciful redeemer, friend and brother, may we know Thee more clearly, love Thee more dearly, and follow Thee more nearly; for Thine own sake.

Loving God completely involves our whole personality—our intellect, emotion, and will. "And you shall love the Lord your God with all your heart, and with all your soul, and with all your mind, and with all your strength" (Mark 12:30). The better we come to know God ("may we know Thee more clearly"), the more we will love Him ("love Thee more dearly"). And the more we love Him, the greater our willingness to trust and obey Him in the things He calls us to do ("follow Thee more nearly").

May We Know Thee More Clearly…

The great prayers in Ephesians 1 and 3, Philippians 1, and Colossians 1 reveal that Paul's deepest desire for his readers was that they grow in the knowledge of Jesus Christ. The knowledge the apostle had in mind was not merely propositional, but personal. He prayed that the Lord would give them a spirit of wisdom and of revelation in the knowledge of Him, that the eyes of their hearts would be enlightened, and that they would know the love of Christ which surpasses knowledge (Ephesians 1:17–18; 3:19).

The occupational hazard of theologians is to become so engrossed in the development of systematic models of understanding that God becomes an abstract intellectual formulation they discuss and write about instead of a living Person they love on bended knees. In the deepest sense, Christianity is not a religion, but a relationship.

When Thomas Aquinas was pressed by his secretary, Reginald of Piperno, to explain why he stopped working on his uncompleted *Summa Theologica,* he said, "All that I have written seems like straw compared to what has now been revealed to me." According to tradition, in his vision he heard the Lord say, "Thomas, you have written well of me: what shall be your reward?" and his reply was, "No reward but Yourself, Lord." Our greatest mental, physical, and social achievements are as straw compared to one glimpse of the living God (Philippians 3:7–10). Our Lord invites us to the highest calling of all—intimacy with Him—and day after day, we decline the offer, preferring instead to fill our stomachs with the pods of short-lived pleasures and prospects.

What does it take to know Him more clearly? The two essential ingredients are time and obedience. It takes time to cultivate a relationship, and unless we make the choice of setting aside consistent time for disciplines such as solitude, silence, prayer, and the reading of Scripture, we will never become intimate with our Lord. Obedience is the proper response to this communication, since it is our personal expression of trust in the promises of the Person we are coming to know.

...Love Thee More Dearly...

To know God is to love Him, because the more we grasp—not merely in our minds but in our experience—who He is and what He has done for us, the more our hearts will respond in love and gratitude. "We love, because He first loved us" (1 John 4:19). When we discover that the personal author of time, space, matter, and energy has, for some incomprehensible reason, chosen to love us to the point of infinite sacrifice, we begin to embrace the unconditional security we longed for all our lives. God's love for us is spontaneous, free, uncaused, and undeserved; He did not set His love on us because we were lovable, beautiful, or clever, because in our sin we were unlovable, ugly, and foolish. He loved us because He *chose* to love us. As we expand our vision of our acceptance and security in Christ who loved us and gave Himself for us, we begin to realize that God is not the enemy of our joy but the source of our joy. It is when we respond to this love that we become the people He has called us to be. By God's grace we need to grow in love with Him in our thoughts, in our emotions, and in our actions.

...Follow Thee More Nearly

As we grow to know and love God, we learn that we can trust His character, promises, and precepts. Whenever He asks us to avoid something, it is not because He is a cosmic killjoy, but because He knows that it is not in our best interests. And whenever He asks us to do something, it is always because it will lead to a greater good. If we are committed to following hard after God, we must do the things He tells us to do. But the risk of obedience is that it will often make no sense to us at the time. It is countercultural to obey the things the Holy Spirit reveals to us in the Scriptures. Radical obedience sometimes flies in the face of human logic, but it is in these times that our loving Father tests and reveals the quality of our trust and dependence on Him. Our great task in the spiritual life is to will to do His will, to love the things He loves, and to choose the things He sets before us for our good.

CHAPTER 2

Relational Spirituality

LOVING OURSELVES CORRECTLY

THE ISSUE OF IDENTITY

A story is told about the American playwright Arthur Miller that illustrates the issue of personal identity. Sitting alone in a bar, Miller was approached by a well-tailored, slightly tipsy fellow who addressed him thus:

"Aren't you Arthur Miller?"
"Why, yes, I am."
"Don't you remember me?"
"Well...your face seems familiar."
"Why, Art, I'm your old buddy Sam! We went to high school together! We went out on double dates!"
"I'm afraid I—"
"I guess you can see I've done all right. Department stores. What do *you* do, Art?"
"Well, I...write."
"Whaddya write?"
"Plays, mostly."
"Ever get any produced?"
"Yes, some."
"Would I know any?"
"Well...perhaps you've heard of *Death of a Salesman?*"
Sam's jaw dropped; his face went white. For a

moment he was speechless. Then he cried out, "Why, you're ARTHUR MILLER!"

(Willard R. Espy, *Another Almanac of Words at Play*)

Sam recognized his high school friend Arthur Miller, and he was familiar with the dramatist Arthur Miller, but he didn't realize the two were one and the same. There is a sense in which this happens in our own experience as believers in Christ—we know ourselves and each other in a superficial way, but we do not really grasp who we are at the core of our being. Like the stories about the man who has forgotten his name, we can wander about the streets of life without knowing our true identity.

WHO DEFINES YOU?

We are constantly in danger of letting the world define us instead of God because it is so easy to do. It is only natural to shape our self-image by the attitudes and opinions of our parents, our peer groups, and our society. None of us are immune to the distorting effects of performance-based acceptance, and we can falsely conclude that we are worthless or that we must try to earn God's acceptance. It is only when we define ourselves by the truths of the Word rather than the thinking and experiences of the world that we can discover our deepest identity.

All of us have encountered a good deal of psychobabble about self-love, including the call to look within ourselves to discover the answers to our problems. But the Scriptures exhort us to look to Christ, and not to self, for the solutions we so greatly need. I have come to define the biblical view of self-love in this way: *loving ourselves correctly means seeing ourselves as God sees us.* This will never happen automatically because the scriptural vision of human depravity and dignity is countercultural. To genuinely believe and embrace the reality of who we have become as a result of our faith in Christ requires consistent discipline and exposure to the Word of God. It also requires a context of fellowship and encouragement in a community of like-minded believers. Without these, the visible will overcome the invisible, and our understanding of this truth will gradually slip through our fingers.

SEEING OURSELVES AS GOD SEES US

What does it mean to see ourselves as God sees us? Contrary to our culture, the biblical doctrine of grace humbles us without degrading us and elevates us without inflating us. It tells us that apart from Christ we have nothing and can do nothing of eternal value. We are spiritually impotent and inadequate without Him, and we must not put our confidence in the flesh (Philippians 3:3). On the other hand, grace also tells us that we have become new creatures in Christ, having been transferred from the kingdom of darkness to the kingdom of His light, life, and love. In Him, we now enjoy complete forgiveness from sins and limitless privileges as unconditionally accepted members of God's family. Our past has been changed because of our new heredity in Christ, and our future is secure because of our new destiny as members of His body.

Thus, a biblical understanding of grace addresses both human depravity and human dignity. It avoids the extreme of "worm" theology (I'm worthless, I'm no good, I'll never amount to anything, I'm nothing but a rotten sinner) and the opposite extreme of pride and autonomy. "What do you have that you did not receive? But if you did receive it, why do you boast as if you had not received it?" (1 Corinthians 4:7). Grace teaches us that the most important thing about us is not what we do but who and whose we are in Christ. *Being is more fundamental than doing;* the better we grasp our identity in Christ, the more our actions will reflect Christlike character.

WHO DOES GOD SAY I AM?

Here is a list of biblical affirmations about our identity in Jesus Christ that is derived from a few selected passages in the New Testament. This is just a portion of the many truths about who we have become through faith in God's Son, but it is a powerful inventory to review from time to time.

♦ I am a child of God.
But as many as received Him, to them He gave the right to become children of God, even to those who believe in His name. (John 1:12)

♦ I am a branch of the true vine, and a conduit of Christ's life.
I am the true vine, and My Father is the vinedresser. I am the vine, you are the branches; he who abides in Me and I in him, he bears much fruit; for apart from Me you can do nothing. (John 15:1, 5)

♦ I am a friend of Jesus.
No longer do I call you slaves, for the slave does not know what his master is doing; but I have called you friends, for all things that I have heard from My Father I have made known to you. (John 15:15)

♦ I have been justified and redeemed.
Being justified as a gift by His grace through the redemption which is in Christ Jesus. (Romans 3:24)

♦ My old self was crucified with Christ, and I am no longer a slave to sin.
Knowing this, that our old self was crucified with Him, that our body of sin might be done away with, that we should no longer be slaves to sin. (Romans 6:6)

♦ I will not be condemned by God.
There is therefore now no condemnation for those who are in Christ Jesus. (Romans 8:1)

♦ I have been set free from the law of sin and death.
For the law of the Spirit of life in Christ Jesus has set you free from the law of sin and of death. (Romans 8:2)

♦ As a child of God, I am a fellow heir with Christ.
*And if children, heirs also, heirs of God and fellow heirs
with Christ, if indeed we suffer with Him in order that we
may also be glorified with Him.* (Romans 8:17)

♦ I have been accepted by Christ.
*Wherefore, accept one another, just as Christ also accepted
us to the glory of God.* (Romans 15:7)

♦ I have been called to be a saint.
*To the church of God which is at Corinth, to those who have
been sanctified in Christ Jesus, saints by calling, with all who
in every place call upon the name of our Lord Jesus Christ,
their Lord and ours.* (1 Corinthians 1:2. See also Ephesians
1:1; Philippians 1:1; Colossians 1:2)

♦ In Christ Jesus, I have wisdom, righteousness, sanctification, and redemption.
*But by His doing you are in Christ Jesus, who became to
us wisdom from God, and righteousness and sanctification, and redemption.* (1 Corinthians 1:30)

♦ My body is a temple of the Holy Spirit who dwells in me.
*Do you not know that you are a temple of God, and that the
Spirit of God dwells in you? (1 Corinthians 3:16)
Or do you not know that your body is a temple of the
Holy Spirit who is in you, whom you have from God, and
that you are not your own? (1 Corinthians 6:19)*

♦ I am joined to the Lord and am one spirit with Him.
*But the one who joins himself to the Lord is one spirit with
Him.* (1 Corinthians 6:17)

♦ God leads me in the triumph and knowledge of Christ.
*But thanks be to God, who always leads us in triumph in
Christ, and manifests through us the sweet aroma of the*

knowledge of Him in every place. (2 Corinthians 2:14)

♦ The hardening of my mind has been removed in Christ.
But their minds were hardened; for until this very day at the reading of the old covenant the same veil remains unlifted, because it is removed in Christ. (2 Corinthians 3:14)

♦ I am a new creature in Christ.
Therefore if any man is in Christ, he is a new creature; the old things passed away; behold, new things have come. (2 Corinthians 5:17)

♦ I have become the righteousness of God in Christ.
He made Him who knew no sin to be sin on our behalf, that we might become the righteousness of God in Him. (2 Corinthians 5:21)

♦ I have been made one with all who are in Christ Jesus.
There is neither Jew nor Greek, there is neither slave nor free man, there is neither male nor female; for you are all one in Christ Jesus. (Galatians 3:28)

♦ I am no longer a slave, but a child and an heir.
Therefore you are no longer a slave, but a son; and if a son, then an heir through God. (Galatians 4:7)

♦ I have been set free in Christ.
It was for freedom that Christ set us free; therefore keep standing firm and do not be subject again to a yoke of slavery. (Galatians 5:1)

♦ I have been blessed with every spiritual blessing in the heavenly places.
Blessed be the God and Father of our Lord Jesus Christ, who has blessed us with every spiritual blessing in the heavenly places in Christ. (Ephesians 1:3)

♦ I am chosen, holy, and blameless before God.
Just as He chose us in Him before the foundation of the world, that we should be holy and blameless before Him. (Ephesians 1:4)

♦ I am redeemed and forgiven by the grace of Christ.
In Him we have redemption through His blood, the forgiveness of our trespasses, according to the riches of His grace. (Ephesians 1:7)

♦ I have been predestined by God to obtain an inheritance.
In Him also we have obtained an inheritance, having been predestined according to His purpose who works all things after the counsel of His will. (Ephesians 1:10–11)

♦ I have been sealed with the Holy Spirit of promise.
In Him, you also, after listening to the message of truth, the gospel of your salvation—having also believed, you were sealed in Him with the Holy Spirit of promise. (Ephesians 1:13)

♦ Because of God's mercy and love, I have been made alive with Christ.
But God, being rich in mercy, because of His great love with which He loved us, even when we were dead in our transgressions, made us alive together with Christ (by grace you have been saved). (Ephesians 2:4–5)

♦ I am seated in the heavenly places with Christ.
And raised us up with Him, and seated us with Him in the heavenly places in Christ Jesus. (Ephesians 2:6)

♦ I am God's workmanship created to produce good works.
For we are His workmanship, created in Christ Jesus for good works, which God prepared beforehand so that we would walk in them. (Ephesians 2:10)

♦ I have been brought near to God by the blood of Christ.
But now in Christ Jesus you who formerly were far off have been brought near by the blood of Christ. (Ephesians 2:13)

♦ I am a member of Christ's body and a partaker of His promise.
The Gentiles are fellow heirs and fellow members of the body, and fellow partakers of the promise in Christ Jesus through the gospel. (Ephesians 3:6)

♦ I have boldness and confident access to God through faith in Christ.
In whom we have boldness and confident access through faith in Him. (Ephesians 3:12)

♦ My new self is righteous and holy.
Put on the new self, which in the likeness of God has been created in righteousness and holiness of the truth. (Ephesians 4:24)

♦ I was formerly darkness, but now I am light in the Lord.
You were formerly darkness, but now you are light in the Lord; walk as children of light. (Ephesians 5:8)

♦ I am a citizen of heaven.
For our citizenship is in heaven, from which also we eagerly wait for a Savior, the Lord Jesus Christ. (Philippians 3:20)

♦ The peace of God guards my heart and mind.
And the peace of God, which surpasses all comprehension, will guard your hearts and your minds in Christ Jesus. (Philippians 4:7)

♦ God supplies all my needs.
And my God shall supply all your needs according to His riches in glory in Christ Jesus. (Philippians 4:19)

♦ I have been made complete in Christ.
In Him you have been made complete, and He is the head over all rule and authority. (Colossians 2:10)

♦ I have been raised up with Christ.
If then you have been raised up with Christ, keep seeking the things above, where Christ is, seated at the right hand of God. (Colossians 3:1)

♦ My life is hidden with Christ in God.
For you have died and your life is hidden with Christ in God. (Colossians 3:3)

♦ Christ is my life, and I will be revealed with Him in glory.
When Christ, who is our life, is revealed, then you also will be revealed with Him in glory. (Colossians 3:4)

♦ I have been chosen of God, and I am holy and beloved.
So, as those who have been chosen of God, holy and beloved, put on a heart of compassion, kindness, humility, gentleness and patience. (Colossians 3:12)

♦ God loves me and has chosen me.
Knowing, brethren beloved by God, His choice of you. (1 Thessalonians 1:4)

The more we embrace these truths from Scripture about who we have become in Christ, the more stable, grateful, and fully assured we will be in this world.

Relational Spirituality

LOVING OTHERS COMPASSIONATELY

FROM THE VERTICAL TO THE HORIZONTAL

We have seen that the purpose for which we were created is an intimate relationship with the infinite and personal God who loves us. He is the initiator of this relationship, and we love Him because He first loved us. Loving God completely is the key to loving self correctly (seeing ourselves as God sees us), and this in turn is the key to loving others compassionately. As we grow in our understanding of God's unconditional love and acceptance of us in Christ, we are increasingly liberated from the selfish quest of using people to meet our needs.

EXPRESSING GOD'S LOVE ON THE HORIZONTAL

This developing vertical relationship of loving the Father, Son, and Holy Spirit will find its manifestations on the horizontal, since there is no act that begins with the love of God that does not end with the love of neighbor. "This is My commandment, that you love one another, just as I have loved you" (John 15:12; cf. 1 John 3:23). "Beloved, let us love one another, for love is from God; and everyone who loves is born of God and knows God. The one who does not love does not know God, for God is love. By this the love of God was manifested in us, that God has sent His only begotten Son into the world so that we might live through Him. In this is love, not that we loved God, but that He loved us and sent His Son to be the propitiation for our sins. Beloved, if God so loved us, we also ought to love one another" (1 John 4:7–11).

Our faith in the work Christ accomplished for us in the past and our hope of the future completion of this work when we see Him are demonstrated in the present through the choices and works of love. The more we love God, the more we will express His transcendent love in other-centered deeds of kindness and goodness.

THE QUEST FOR GREATNESS IN THE SIGHT OF MEN

Near the end of our Lord's earthly ministry, His disciples were arguing about who would occupy the best positions in His kingdom. They refused to listen to His increasingly frequent words about His coming crucifixion and focused instead on the part they wanted to hear. When James and John approached Jesus and said, "Grant that we may sit, one on Your right and one on Your left, in Your glory" (Mark 10:37), the other disciples became indignant because they had their eyes on the same places. Jesus told them that the one who wishes to be great among them will be their servant, and whoever wishes to be first among them will be slave of all. "For even the Son of Man did not come to be served, but to serve, and to give His life a ransom for many" (Mark 10:43–45).

Weeks later when Jesus celebrated the Passover with His disciples on the night before His own sacrifice, the same dispute surfaced again. Christ's rebuttal to their quest for recognition was that true greatness is found in those who are willing to serve. "For who is greater, the one who reclines at the table or the one who serves? Is it not the one who reclines at the table? But I am among you as the one who serves" (Luke 22:27).

THE ESSENCE OF TRUE GREATNESS

John 13 portrays a visual parable that communicated this precise issue to the disciples with poignancy and clarity. It is evident that there was no servant to wash the feet of the Lord and His men before they reclined at the table. This must have been an embarrassing situation: foot washing was a customary part of hospitality in the ancient Near East, but it was obvious that if the disciples were fighting for their place in the sun, none of them would volunteer to be the servant of all. Their embarrassment became acute when Jesus Himself rose from supper, laid aside His garments, tied a towel around Himself, and began to wash the disciples' feet and wipe them with the towel. His lesson was evident: if their Teacher and Lord became their servant, they should also serve one another (John 13:13–15).

The key to Christ's willingness to serve others in place of being served by them is found in the crucial truth that Jesus knew that "the Father had given all things into His hands, and that He had come forth from God and was going back to God" (John 13:3). He knew His dignity and power ("the Father had given all things into His hands"), He knew His significance and identity ("and that He had come forth from God"), and He knew His security and destiny ("and was going back to God").

It is important to note that Jesus derived His identity from His relationship with His Father and not from the opinions of His family and peers. Consider these passages:

- ◆ "Can any good thing come out of Nazareth?" (John 1:46).
- ◆ "Why is He eating and drinking with tax collectors and sinners?" (Mark 2:16).
- ◆ "Is not this the carpenter, the son of Mary, and brother of James and Joses and Judas and Simon? Are not His sisters here with us?" And they took offense at Him (Mark 6:3).
- ◆ "The Son of Man came eating and drinking, and they say, 'Behold, a gluttonous man and a drunkard, a friend of tax collectors and sinners!'" (Matthew 11:19).
- ◆ "If You do these things, show Yourself to the world." For not even His brothers were believing in Him (John 7:4–5).
- ◆ They said to Him, "We were not born of fornication" (John 8:41).

♦ The Jews answered and said to Him, "Do we not say rightly that You are a Samaritan and have a demon?" (John 8:48).

♦ When He left there, the scribes and the Pharisees began to be very hostile and to question Him closely on many subjects, plotting against Him to catch Him in something He might say (Luke 11:53–54).

Jesus was criticized, rejected, slandered, misunderstood, plotted against, betrayed, denied, and abused by His family and friends, His disciples, the Jewish religious leaders, and the Romans. As His ministry progressed, our Lord faced increasing levels of hostility and opposition. In spite of all this, He knew who and whose He was, and His relationship with the Father gave Him the power and security to love and serve others. It would have been impossible for Jesus to have done this if He had allowed Himself to be defined and bound by the opinions of the people around Him.

CHRIST'S RESOURCES ARE OUR RESOURCES

Just as Jesus knew who He was, where He came from, and where He was going, so all who have put their trust and hope in Him should know the same. But few do. It is only as we frequently renew our minds with the spiritual truth of the Scriptures that we will move our thinking into alignment with the reality of who we are in Christ. Like Christ, we have dignity and power; every spiritual blessing has been given into our hands (Ephesians 1:3, 19; 3:16, 20–21). We also have significance and identity; we have become the children of God (Romans 8:16; 1 John 3:1–2). And we have been given the security and destiny of knowing that nothing can separate us from the love of God in Christ (Romans 8:18, 35–39). These limitless resources meet our deepest needs and overcome the human dilemma of loneliness, insignificance, and meaninglessness.

When these truths begin to define our self-image, they make

us *secure enough to love and serve others* without seeking our own interests first. Because of our security and significance in Christ, we do not need to be controlled by the opinions and responses of others. We have nothing to prove because we know who and whose we are. Rather than trying to impress and manipulate people, we can do our work with excellence as unto the Lord (Colossians 3:23). The more we are concerned with what God thinks of us, the less we will be worried about what others think of us. And when we are no longer enslaved to people's opinions of us, we are free to love and serve them as Christ loves us—with no strings attached.

THE RISKS AND REWARDS OF RELATIONSHIPS

As these truths about what God has already accomplished for us become clearer in our thinking, we grow in awareness of our true freedom in Christ and desire to express this freedom and security in the way we approach relationships. Instead of one-upmanship, we can actually enjoy our membership in "the order of the towel" by taking pleasure in putting others first. Our *identification* with Christ leads to and is the basis for our *imitation* of Christ. This is precisely what Paul invited the Philippians to do when he told them to "do nothing from selfishness or empty conceit, but with humility of mind regard one another as more important than yourselves; do not merely look out for your own personal interests, but also for the interests of others" (Philippians 2:3–4). The apostle then used the servanthood of Jesus as the model for the mind-set that we as His servants should embrace in our service to others (see 2:5–8).

But it is one thing to exalt the virtues of being a servant and another to be treated as one. It requires the sufficiency and security of a growing realization of our identification with Jesus Christ to minister with other-centered concern to people who misunderstand us and may never respect us. We will frequently need to review the truth that our performance and our acceptance by other people has nothing to do with our dignity and value, since this is determined by God and not by the world. When we suffer rejection and indifference, the pain will be very real, but it need not destroy us, since we have made the radical decision to look to God and His resources alone for our true and unchanging identity and worth.

If I had to choose one word to summarize the theme of the Bible from Genesis to Revelation, that word would be *relationships*. We have seen that God is a community of being—in the mystery of the divine Trinity, the three Persons of the Godhead enjoy perfect mutual love. We have also seen that God created us in His image as relational beings whose ultimate source of fullness and enjoyment should have been found in fellowship and intimacy with God. Through His loving initiative, God has overcome the alienation and separation caused by human sin by sending His Son into the world to pay for our guilt and to give us His life. The restoration of our vertical relationship with God that was made possible through Christ's atonement now becomes the basis for the restoration of righteous horizontal relationships with others. (Righteousness in Scripture is a relational concept, since it refers to good, just, and loving associations with God and others.)

As children of God through faith in Christ, we are called to a lifestyle of growing other-centeredness and diminishing self-centeredness as Christ increases and we decrease. While we are aware that in a sinful world, such a lifestyle makes us more vulnerable to the pains of rejection, indifference, demands, misunderstanding, and betrayal, we also realize that a wise person finds more joy in serving others than in pursuing possessions, power, performance, or prestige. Both the Old and the New Testaments resonate with this theme, and repeatedly tell us that a vital vertical relationship with the Lord is the key to quality horizontal relationships with others. The apostle Paul exemplified this wisdom when he described his Philippian readers as "my joy and crown" (4:1) and encouraged them to "rejoice in the Lord always; again I will say, rejoice!" (4:4). The Lord should be the ultimate source of our joy and the continual source of our joy, whether our circumstances and dealings with people are positive or negative.

The more we take pleasure in loving and serving God, the greater our capacity to take pleasure in loving and serving people.

Thus, Paul could write to the Thessalonians, "For who is our hope or joy or crown of exultation? Is it not even you, in the presence of our Lord Jesus at His coming? For you are our glory and joy" (1 Thessalonians 2:19–20; cf. 3:9). When we are secure in Christ, the rewards of investing our lives in people exceed the pains that people can cause. Paul not only saw people as a source of joy, but also as a *reward*, both in the present and in the future. When we love and serve people with eternal values in mind, there is great reward in being part of the process of people coming to Christ and growing in their character and relationships with their mates, children, and associates. There is joy in being used of God in encouraging, comforting, and building up others in our arenas of influence.

Jonathan Edwards observed that the ultimate good in life is to treat things according to their true value. The converse is also true, and we face the ever-present danger of treating the eternal as though it were temporal and the temporal as though it were eternal. The world system switches the price tags and encourages us to pursue things that will not last. "That which is highly esteemed among men is detestable in the sight of God" (Luke 16:15b). If we really want to be rich toward God (Luke 12:21), we must give our lives in exchange for the things God declares to be important.

The heart always provides for what it values (Matthew 6:19–34), and if we value God first, our capacity to love Him and others will expand. If we value the world first, we will not only miss out on the joys of knowing God, but also the joys of this present life. Relationships will degenerate into contacts, and we will seek to manipulate people to get what we think we want. We will be driven to accomplish and impress, and this will detract from quality time with those we really love. Activities will easily take precedence over intimacy, both with God and with people. The idol of accomplishment will erode the aesthetics of the spirit and leave us busy and weary. We will work harder to influence people, and by seeking our security in their responses, we will become disconnected from our true security in Christ. The only way off this treadmill is repentance and return to the pursuit of Christ in place of the pursuit of the world.

It has been said that "everyone ought to fear to die until he has done something that will last forever." These are strong words, but they deserve serious consideration, as does this statement that has been attributed to Joan of Arc: "It is not a tragedy to die for something you believe in, but it is a tragedy to find at the end of your life that what you believed in betrayed you." This thought captures the essence of our ongoing struggle between the claims of the temporal and those of the eternal. Scripture repeatedly reminds us that "the world is passing away, and also its lusts; but the one who does the will of God lives forever" (1 John 2:17). This planet is transitory: when the day of the Lord comes like a thief, "the earth and its works will be burned up" (2 Peter 3:10). Yet something in us longs for the eternal, for that which will not pass away. We cannot satisfy this longing through earthly accomplishments, naming buildings and land after ourselves, building corporate empires, collecting valued possessions, or other forms of human endeavor, because all of these things are destined to disappear. What, then, can we do on this planet that will always live? What can give permanence to the work of our hands (Psalm 90:17)? The answer lies in the biblical truth that after their fleeting years on earth, people go on into eternity. When we invite Christ to manifest His life in and through us, when we represent the Lord Jesus in our spheres of influence and encourage others to know Him better, we are investing in something that transcends this planet.

This should be our prayer for ourselves and for those who enter into our sphere of influence. All of us want to do something that will endure—it is frightening to think that we could run life's course in vain, ending up without a single work that will live on beyond the grave. But the Lord Jesus has promised that when we allow Him to accomplish His work in and through us, the results will last forever. We cannot take our earthly possessions with us, but according to the gospel, we can take people with us. We bring nothing into this world, and we can take nothing material out of it. But if we are investing in the lives of people, our investments will accrue dividends forever, since people were made in the image of God to inhabit eternity.

FIVE KINDS OF PEOPLE

In his helpful book *Restoring Your Spiritual Passion,* Gordon MacDonald observes that there are five kinds of people that we encounter. First, there are the very resourceful people (VRPs), who add to our lives and ignite our passion. These are mentors, and they are often older men or women who are willing to build their experience and wisdom into our lives. It is wise to search for such people prayerfully, since they are less likely to search for us. Second, there are the very important people (VIPs), who share our passion. These people love us enough to ask us tough questions and keep us honest as they work together with us and share our vision. Third, there are the very trainable people (VTPs), who catch our passion, and these are people newer to the faith in whose lives we have been called to make an investment. These three groups correspond in turn to Paul, Barnabas, and Timothy, and we need exposure to all three for spiritual growth and reproduction.

Fourth, there are what MacDonald calls the very nice people (VNPs), who enjoy our passion but do not contribute to it. These people make up the large majority of congregations in the relatively unpersecuted Western churches, and most church programs focus on accommodating them and their needs. Finally, there are the very draining people (VDPs), who sap our passion by causing conflicts and constantly looking for comfort and recognition. If we are not careful, the VNPs and VDPs we encounter will absorb the majority of our available time. This does not mean that we should not treat them with dignity and compassion, especially since it is possible for such people to change when they become open to the ministry of the Holy Spirit in their lives. Jesus indeed ministered to those who were sick, suffering, curious, and critical, but He spent the majority of His time with His Father and with His disciples. In the same way, we can protect ourselves from difficult people without writing them off. We have all encountered people who seem to be one taco short of a combination plate, but by the grace of God, it is possible for a VDP to become a VRP.

THE GRACE OF FORGIVENESS

One of the most important dynamics in relational spirituality is the grace of forgiveness.

Forgiven by God

It has been observed that there is no sin so great that God will not forgive, but there is no sin so small that it does not need to be forgiven. The Old and New Testaments center on the theme of redemption and forgiveness, stressing the human condition as one of alienation and moral guilt before the holiness of the Creator. It is through God's mighty and loving act of redemption in the cross of Christ that He can offer the gracious gift of forgiveness without compromising the perfection of His justice and character. And it is through the grace of divine forgiveness that our alienation can be overcome and a loving, secure relationship as true members of God's family can be inaugurated.

The dynamic of forgiveness involves the response of repentance and confession. We must humble ourselves before God and admit the reality of our sinfulness, asking Him for the gift of forgiveness and new life in Christ. And having put our trust in Christ alone for our salvation, we stay in fellowship with Him by asking the Spirit to search our hearts and reveal any areas of unconfessed sin, and responding by acknowledging these to the Lord and thanking Him for His forgiveness (Psalm 139:23–24; 1 John 1:9).

God's forgiveness erases the sin from existence: in the imagery from the Old Testament, He removes it "as far as the east is from the west" (Psalm 103:12), He casts them behind His back (Isaiah 38:17), He wipes out our transgressions for His own sake (Isaiah 43:25), He remembers our sin no more (Jeremiah 31:34), and He casts all our sins into the depths of the sea (Micah 7:19). In the imagery of the New Testament, we are assured that "when you were dead in your transgressions and the uncircumcision of your flesh, He made you alive together with Him, having forgiven us all our transgressions, having canceled out the certificate of debt consisting of decrees against us, which was hostile to us; and He has taken it out of the way, having nailed it to the cross" (Colossians 2:13–14).

Even after coming to Christ, many people find it difficult to accept God's unconditional forgiveness. There is still a lingering natural disposition to think we must work off the debt and earn divine forgiveness. Guilt feelings can cause people to revisit the sin in the past instead of laying hold of the fact of God's forgiveness in the present. The idea that we have outsinned the grace of God is a failure to grasp the height and depth of God's grace and love.

Forgiving Others

> I was angry with my foe:
> I told it not, my wrath did grow.
> WILLIAM BLAKE

Having been forgiven by the grace of God on the basis of Christ's finished work on the cross, we are now exhorted to manifest a mind-set of forgiveness in our relationships with others (see Matthew 18:21–35). Thus Paul exhorts us to "be kind to one another, tender-hearted, forgiving each other, just as God in Christ also has forgiven you" (Ephesians 4:32; cf. Matthew 5:12). Elsewhere he writes: "So, as those who have been chosen of God, holy and beloved, put on a heart of compassion, kindness, humility, gentleness and patience; bearing with one another, and forgiving each other, whoever has a complaint against anyone; just as the Lord forgave you, so also should you. Beyond all these things put on love, which is the perfect bond of unity. Let the peace of Christ rule in your hearts, to which indeed you were called in one body; and be thankful" (Colossians 3:12–15).

The Cost of Forgiveness

When we forgive those who have hurt us, we are really acknowledging that we too have needed forgiveness and that we are not as different from the offender as we might like to think. There is a natural tendency in all of us to excuse our own faults and to blame others for their faults, an inclination to reach for grace and understanding in our own situation and to reach for justice and possibly revenge when the same wrong is committed by others.

Instead, Scripture calls us, as people who have experienced God's forgiveness, to take the place of the other person.

In Christ, we are to offer grace rather than justice to the wrongdoer (*charizomai*, one of the words used in the New Testament for forgiveness, means "to deal graciously with"; notice how it is used in 2 Corinthians 2:6–8). This is often a difficult and unnatural act, because it does not seem fair to those who have been wronged. For to forgive others is to release them from any obligation to make up to you what they have taken from you. But as Lewis B. Smedes argues in *Forgive and Forget*, "When you release the wrongdoer from the wrong, you cut a malignant tumor out of your inner life. You set a prisoner free, but you discover that the real prisoner was yourself."

Thus, to forgive as we have been forgiven by God is really an act of faith, since it means that we are releasing the right to resentment and we are entrusting justice to God rather than seeking it ourselves (see Romans 12:19). To forgive is to act on the truth that it is only God and not we who can change another person.

It has been quipped that "There's no point in burying a hatchet if you're going to put a marker on the site." But when we have been seriously injured by another, we want to put a marker on the site so that we can dig our resentments up to nurse them from time to time. Because forgiveness can feel like outrageous injustice, it can be a lengthy process rather than a once-for-all event. This is evident in the painful process Joseph went through in forgiving his treacherous brothers (Genesis 42–45).

Long after you have forgiven, the wound can linger on in your memory. As Smedes observes, forgiving is not the same as forgetting or excusing or smoothing things over. True forgiveness is costly, especially when there is no repentance on the part of the wrongdoer. But it is only way to release us and others from the bondage of guilt (see Christ's gracious restoration of Peter in John 21:15–19) and to break the vicious cycle of blame. Part of the cost is letting loose of the pride that can allow trivial things to corrode a relationship for years or decades.

As an exercise before God, take a piece of paper and write

down the names of those who have hurt you over the years through disloyalty and betrayal. Offer this list to God along with all the pain it rekindles, and make a choice through faith in Christ to forgive each person on the list. Then crumple the paper and burn it before the Lord who forgave you from the cross.

HOW LONG WILL IT LAST?

I have attended a number of funerals in the past few years, and the difference between funerals for believers and unbelievers is the difference between day and night, between heaven and earth, and between hope and despair. The "homecoming" ceremony for a person who knew Jesus Christ is a time when our hope in Christ has a true "payoff." We discover that our faith is more real and powerful during these pivotal times when we are forced to acknowledge our lack of control. For a follower of Christ, death is not the end, but the doorway to a new and greater domain. The body is left behind, but the spirit is in the presence of the Lord until the day when it is joined to a new and glorified resurrection body. Scripture assures us that when we are absent from the body, we will be at home with the Lord (2 Corinthians 5:6–7), and it comforts us with the truth that "God will bring with Him those who have fallen asleep in Jesus" and that "the dead in Christ shall rise first. Then we who are alive and remain will be caught up together with them in the clouds to meet the Lord in the air, and so we shall always be with the Lord" (1 Thessalonians 4:13–18).

When a loved one irrevocably departs this life, there are far-reaching implications that extend into the three dimensions of time.

Past

Whenever I hear of the passing of someone I knew and loved, a flood of memories surge into my consciousness. Images of the person's life multiply, flashing across the screen of my mind in such a way that I can see all the years of my relationship with the person simultaneously. In times like this, the mind seems to search for and collect all the treasures and troubles and display them in a vivid array that forces one to realize the impact of the other's life as though for the first time. And I discover not only how much I was shaped by that impact, but also the truth that this person took a real part of me away with him or her. For there were certain responses and facets of my personality that only this person could elicit. Those unique behaviors are inert with anyone else.

Present

The influence of significant others creates ripple effects that continue to touch our lives long after these people are gone. We cannot measure the repercussions because they keep compounding and reverberating in subtle ways through the years and generations. The fullness of this process will not be evident until the day of Christ, but it reminds us once again that each of us is called to the present process of fulfilling God's unique purpose for us during the few years of our earthly sojourn.

Another implication for the present is the importance of treating each relationship as though it could be our last contact. This kind of closure would produce a lifestyle of few regrets, because it would mean that we do not leave behind any unfinished business such as speaking our love, forgiving and asking forgiveness, or expressing our gratitude for all the other person has done and meant.

Future

The passing of one who is beloved is a reminder of our own mortality and of the brevity of our pilgrimage in the world. Ecclesiastes 7:2 tells us that "It is better to go to a house of mourning than to go to a house of feasting, because that is the end of every man, and the living takes it to heart." Funerals are memorandums of reality, and for a time, they open a window of vulnerability to the truth of the temporal versus the eternal. While our defenses and diversions are down, they invite us to answer the question, "Where is my hope? Am I hoping in the promises and rewards of the world, or am I laying hold of a hope that will never fade or disappoint?" Scripture tells us that those who put their hope in Christ will not be disappointed (Romans 9:33). This hope is an anchor of the soul (Hebrews 6:19) and it strengthens the believer to remain steadfast during the tempests of life.

———

Paradigm Spirituality

L I F E   I S   A   J O U R N E Y,
B U T   W H E R E   A R E   W E   G O I N G ?

O N E   Y E A R   T O   L I V E

Suppose your doctor tells you, after a routine physical examination, that you have a terminal illness. You seek a second and third opinion, and all agree that at best you have one year to live. There will be no discernible effects of the disease until it has reached its course.

How would this scenario affect your vision of life, your roles on this earth, and the way you should invest your remaining time? The degree to which it would alter your present perspective and practice is the distance between your current view of life and the biblical view of life. The latter emphasizes the brevity of our earthly sojourn and stresses the urgency of investing our most precious asset, time, in a way that will have lasting consequences. The former view typically denies the imminence of death and, for all practical purposes, treats the temporal as though it were eternal.

A   G R A S P   O F   L I F E ' S   B R E V I T Y

Time, like an ever-rolling stream,
Bears all its sons away;
They fly forgotten as a dream
Dies at the op'ning day.

The busy tribes of flesh and blood
With all their cares and fears,
Are carried downward like a flood
And lost in following years.

These verses from Isaac Watts's hymn "O God, Our Help in Ages Past" are based on the profound contrast in Psalm 90 between the eternality of God and the brevity of our earthly sojourn. This psalm, written by Moses near the end of his own journey, counsels us to number our days in order to present to God a heart of wisdom (v. 12). David's meditation in Psalm 39:4–7 develops the same theme:

LORD, make me to know my end,
And what is the extent of my days,
Let me know how transient I am.
Behold, Thou hast made my days as handbreadths,
And my lifetime as nothing in Thy sight,
Surely every man at his best is a mere breath.
Surely every man walks about as a phantom;
Surely they make an uproar for nothing;
He amasses riches, and does not know who will gather them.
And now, Lord, for what do I wait?
My hope is in Thee.

Isaiah 40:6b–8 uses a different metaphor to develop the radical contrast between the temporal and the eternal (see also Psalm 103:15–18 and 1 Peter 1:24–25):

All flesh is grass, and all its loveliness is like the flower of
    the field.
The grass withers, the flower fades,
When the breath of the Lord blows upon it;
Surely the people are grass.
The grass withers, the flower fades,
But the word of our God stands forever.

James adds this sobering thought: "You do not know what your life will be like tomorrow. You are just a vapor that appears for a little while and then vanishes away" (4:14; cf. 1:11).

BIBLICAL REALISM AND HOPE

Again and again, the Scriptures drive these images home to remind us that our stay on this planet is briefer than most of us are inclined to think. This may seem to be a pessimistic and morbid way of viewing human life, but upon further analysis, it turns out to be a realistic and hopeful approach. It is realistic because it is better to know things as they are than to believe things as they seem. It does not require divine revelation to realize that one out of one dies, and that our few decades of life on earth last no longer than the flower of a field in relation to the many generations that come and go.

It comes as no surprise to see this perspective as realistic, but it is surprising to discover that it is also hopeful. It is hopeful precisely because it informs us that there is more to life than what we presently see, and it assures us that our longing for more than this world can offer is not merely a pipe dream. The biblical vision of God's invitation to us is not only forgiveness, but newness of life in Christ, a new quality of relational life that will never fade or tarnish.

There are three dominant worldviews that are vying for our allegiance. The first of these claims that ultimate reality is material, and that everything in the universe is the impersonal product of time and chance. There are variations of this view, but it is best known as naturalism, atheism, and humanism.

The second worldview claims that ultimate reality is not material, but spiritual. However, this spiritual agent is not a personal being, but the all-that-is. Variations of this view include monism, pantheism, transcendentalism, and the whole New Age movement.

Theism, the third worldview, distinguishes between the creation and the Creator and declares that ultimate reality is an infinite, intelligent, and personal Being. Christian theism affirms that this personal God has decisively revealed Himself in the person and work of Jesus Christ.

Only the third worldview offers genuine hope beyond the grave, since the first predicts annihilation and the second, reincarnation. Contrary to the pop version of reincarnation in the west, the religions of the east teach that reincarnation is undesirable, since it brings us around and around on the painful wheel of life. Instead, the eastern vision of salvation is absorption into the ocean of being. But this is not a vision of personal consciousness or relationships; it is simply a spiritual version of annihilation.

Instead of annihilation or reincarnation, the Scriptures teach resurrection into an eternally new existence of light, life, and love characterized by intimacy with our Lord and with one another. Everything we go through now will be more than worth it in the end, because the divine Architect of the universe, the God and Father of our Lord Jesus Christ, never builds a staircase that leads to nowhere.

TWO COMPETING PARADIGMS

A paradigm is a way of seeing based on implicit or explicit rules that shape one's perspective. A paradigm shift takes place when the rules or boundaries change, so that we no longer see things from the same perspective; when the rules change, our way of seeing is altered. The most celebrated example of a paradigm shift is the Copernican revolution in astronomy. Until the time of Copernicus, the reigning paradigm was Ptolemy's geocentric system; the sun and planets were thought to orbit the earth. For centuries, astronomers held to this Ptolemaic way of viewing the solar system in spite of the fact that a number of observations did not fit this model. But instead of questioning the paradigm, astronomers invented complicated theories of epicycles to explain why some planets appeared to stop, go backward for a while, and then resume their original direction. Copernicus's breakthrough was the realization that all of these observations make perfect sense by switching from a geocentric to a heliocentric (sun-centered) view of the sun and planets—in other words, we do not live in an terrestrial system, but in a solar system. Copernicus realized that this radical shift would meet with a hostile response, especially by those in the religious establishment. His views were published posthumously.

In a similar way, the temporal and eternal perspectives are competing paradigms of life. We can live as if this world is all there is, or we can view our earthly existence as a brief pilgrimage designed to prepare us for eternity. The men and women in Hebrews 11 embraced the latter perspective: "All these died in faith, without receiving the promises, but having seen them and having welcomed them from a distance, and having confessed that they were strangers and exiles on the earth" (Hebrews 11:13). By contrast, those who adopt a temporal paradigm treat the temporal as though it were eternal and the eternal as though it were temporal.

Suppose someone plans to move from Dallas to Atlanta where he knows he will spend the remaining fifty years of his life. He carefully prepares for the two-day drive by poring over every detail of the journey, including what clothing he will wear, what rest stops he will use, where he will refuel his car, what motel he will stay at, all meals he will eat, and where he will eat them. Nothing on the journey is left to chance, but he doesn't have a clue as to what he will do when he arrives in Atlanta. The absurdity of this scenario is easy to see, and yet the bulk of people we encounter are really living their lives in this way. For in this analogy, the two-day trip is our earthly sojourn, and the fifty-year stay is our eternal destiny. But what is obviously ludicrous on a temporal scale somehow seems acceptable when we speak of eternity, perhaps because our eternal destiny seems so vague and wispy to many of us.

Marcel Proust observed that "the real act of discovery consists not in finding new lands but in seeing with new eyes." The problem is that we have been captured by a temporal paradigm because we live in a temporal arena. It takes great risk to shift to a biblical paradigm, because it challenges everything that our culture reinforces. The more we have invested in the cultural paradigm and the better we are at functioning within it, the more we think we may lose by changing to the biblical paradigm. It is only when we renew our minds with biblical truth and reinforce this truth through relationships with other children of the kingdom that we begin to see that we really are on a very brief pilgrimage indeed. When we see this, we discover that we must pursue the things that will last rather than the things that are passing away. The problem is that this temporal/eternal shift, unlike the Copernican revolution in astronomy, is reversible; we can flip-flop back and forth between these opposing perspectives. This is an ongoing struggle that we can expect to encounter for the remainder of our worldly sojourn.

"A SHORT AND FEVERED REHEARSAL"

Prospero, a magician who rules an enchanted island, is the protagonist of Shakespeare's last play, *The Tempest*. When Prospero addresses his guest Ferdinand in the fourth act, it is as though Shakespeare himself, nearing the end of his life, reflects directly through his character:

> Our revels now are ended. These our actors,
> As I foretold you, were all spirits and
> Are melted into air, into thin air;
> And, like the baseless fabric of this vision,
> The cloud-capped towers, the gorgeous palaces,
> The solemn temples, the great globe itself,
> Yea, all which it inherit, shall dissolve,
> And, like this insubstantial pageant faded,
> Leave not a rack behind. We are such stuff
> As dreams are made on, and our little life
> Is rounded with a sleep.

At the end of the play, Prospero gives up his magic and turns his thoughts to the grave. Just so, the playwright would create no more works on the stage of life; reflecting on the brevity of earthly existence, he also understood that the temporal achievements of humanity as a whole would come to an end. This is consistent with the biblical vision of the fiery consumption of all human attainments on the day of God. "But the day of the Lord will come like a thief, in which the heavens will pass away with a roar and the elements will be destroyed with intense heat, and the earth and its works will be burned up" (2 Peter 3:10).

If we examine the heart's deepest longings, it becomes evident that these aspirations cannot be satisfied by any of the offerings of this transitory world. There is insufficient time, opportunity, and energy even to scratch the surface of our deep-seated hopes and dreams. A. W. Tozer put it well in his devotional classic *The Knowledge of the Holy:* "The days of the years of our lives are few, and swifter than a weaver's shuttle. Life is a short and fevered rehearsal for a concert we cannot stay to give. Just when we appear to have attained some proficiency we are forced to lay our instruments down. There is simply not time enough to think, to become, to perform what the constitution of our natures indicates we are capable of."

EXPERIENCING OUR MORTALITY

Few people attain this wisdom in the first three decades of life. In the film *Dead Poets Society,* Robin Williams plays an English teacher in a private school who makes a dramatic attempt at the near-impossible task of communicating this truth to a group of adolescents. He gathers the students before an old trophy case and invites them to look closely at the faces of an earlier class that graduated some seventy or eighty years before. As the camera slowly pans in to a close-up of the faces in the photograph, we see all the hope and ambition of youth in their eyes and smiles. In the voice-over, Williams tells his students that the people in the photo were just like them, but now they are pushing up daisies. He exhorts them to seize the moment—carpe diem!

But it usually requires the sobering struggle of the midlife crisis (or midlife process, depending on the way we go through it) before we experientially grasp our mortality. As we discover the decline of our capacities and the increase of our responsibilities, we realize with clarity and force that we will not be able to fulfill many of our earthly hopes and dreams. This can be traumatic for those whose expectations are limited to this planet, but for believers whose hope is in the character and promises of God, it can be a powerful reminder to transfer their affections and ambitions to their only true home, the kingdom of heaven.

Tozer goes on to add this important thought: "How completely satisfying to turn from our limitations to a God who has none. Eternal years lie in His heart. For Him time does not pass, it remains; and those who are in Christ share with Him all the riches of limitless time and endless years."

The responsibilities and pressures of this world clamor for our attention and tend to squeeze out our inner lives and starve our souls. When this happens, we lose sight of the things that really matter and focus on the things that are passing away. Our value systems become confused when we invest more of our thought and concern in things that are doomed to disappear than in that which will endure forever.

The apostle John warns us of this when he writes, "Do not love the world, nor the things in the world. If anyone loves the world, the love of the Father is not in him. For all that is in the world, the lust of the flesh and the lust of the eyes and the boastful pride of life, is not from the Father, but is from the world. And the world is passing away, and also its lusts; but the one who does the will of God abides forever" (1 John 2:15–17). James adds, "Whoever wishes to be a friend of the world makes himself an enemy of God" (James 4:4). And Jesus admonishes those who are more concerned with the opinions of men than the approval of God, saying, "That which is highly esteemed among men is detestable in the sight of God" (Luke 16:15). These are indeed strong words, but we would be foolish to disregard them. As Augustine wrote, we must care for our bodies as though we were going to live forever, but we must care for our souls as if we were going to die tomorrow.

THE PRECIOUS PRESENT

Does this mean that we should be so heavenly minded that we are of no earthly good? In actual fact, it is precisely the opposite—when people become heavenly minded, they treasure the passing opportunities of this life and become more alive to the present moment. Rather than being overwhelmed with the problems and hassles of life, they understand that these too will pass, and that "the sufferings of this present time are not worthy to be compared with the glory that is to be revealed to us" (Romans 8:18). Instead of taking things for granted, they learn to savor blessings and joys that are otherwise overlooked.

Thornton Wilder portrays this so well in *Our Town,* a play depicting a young woman who, after dying in childbirth, joins the dead in a hillside cemetery. In the third act, the Stage Manager allows Emily to go back and observe a single day of her brief life, but the dead advise her to "choose the least important day in your life. It will be important enough." Emily selects her twelfth birthday, and is soon overwhelmed by the experience.

"I can't. I can't go on. It goes so fast. We don't have time to look at one another....

"I didn't realize. So all that was going on and we never noticed. Take me back—up the hill—to my grave. But first: Wait! One more look.

"Good-by, Good-by, world. Good-by, Grover's Corners...Mama and Papa. Good-by to clocks ticking...and Mama's sunflowers. And food and coffee. And new-ironed dresses and hot baths...and sleeping and waking up. Oh, earth, you're too wonderful for anybody to realize you." She looks toward the Stage Manager and asks abruptly, through her tears:

"Do any human beings ever realize life while they live it?—every, every minute?"

The Stage Manager answers, "No.... The saints and poets, maybe—they do some."

Instead of wasting time as though we had a million years to live on earth, we would do well to remember the apostle Paul's exhortation: "Be most careful then how you conduct yourselves: like sensible men, not like simpletons. Use the present opportunity to the full, for these are evil days. So do not be fools, but try to understand what the will of the Lord is" (Ephesians 5:15–17, NEB).

Eubie Blake, who smoked from the age of six and refused to drink water, was reputed to say after his hundreth birthday, "If I'd known I was going to live this long, I'd have taken better care of myself." When elderly people are asked what they would change if they had another opportunity to go through life, their answers are generally more illuminating than this. Many say that they would reflect more, risk more, and do more things that would last.

I have squandered more money and time on toys and diversions than I would like to tell. We are allotted only a few years to labor in this vineyard. Are we squandering or investing the precious resources of time, talent, and treasure which have been entrusted to us by our heavenly Master?

Paradigm Spirituality

Can We Trust God?

The Risk of Letting Loose

Any attempt to pursue both the claims of the temporal and the eternal is like holding on to two horses that are galloping in opposite directions. The simultaneous pursuit of the kingdom of the world and the kingdom of Christ is impossible—at any point, one or the other will prevail. Many have tried to have it both ways, but this can never be more than a matter of adding a thin spiritual veneer over the same furniture that is manufactured and promoted by the world system.

It takes great risk to let loose of everything we have been taught to clamor after and control. It is never comfortable or natural to treasure the invisible over the visible, the promises of God over the promises of the world, the things that will not be fulfilled until the return of Christ over the things the world says we can have here and now. We want control and security on our own terms, yet the Scriptures tell us that the only true security comes from abandoning the illusion of control and surrendering ourselves unreservedly to the Person and purposes of God.

Two Rival Value Systems

The temporal value system (TVS) demands no trust and dependence upon God because it is based on what is seen; the eternal value system (EVS), on the other hand, is unseen and therefore requires a walk of faith (2 Corinthians 5:7). "For in hope we have been saved, but hope that is seen is not hope; for why does one also hope for what he sees? But if we hope for what we do not see, with perseverance we wait eagerly for it" (Romans 8:24–25).

Our culture bombards us with the mentality that this world is all there is and tells us, in effect, that the goal of life is: "Maximize your pleasure and minimize your pain. Build a name for yourself if you can, and establish a progeny." There are many variations, but the enticing wisdom of this world, as observed by the preacher in Ecclesiastes, is always derived from what is "under the sun." The wisdom which comes from above, from beyond the sun, tells us that we are immortal creatures and that this brief moment on this planet is as nothing compared to the eternal existence that awaits us.

James tells us that there is a warfare between an earthly and demonic wisdom and a heavenly and divine wisdom (James 3:13–17). Each of us is required to make a choice. Which will we believe? How consistent is our behavior with our belief?

In this warfare, TVS promotes pleasure as an end in itself. It implies that people who are willing to forgo earthly pleasures in their pursuit of the ways of God are missing out on "the good life." EVS says that knowing God is the greatest pleasure of all. God Himself is the Source of true pleasure; by comparison, everything else is a shadow.

TVS exalts recognition and the approval of people. EVS exhorts us to desire the approval of God above that of people. "For am I now seeking the favor of men, or of God? Or am I striving to please men? If I were still trying to please men, I would not be a bond-servant of Christ" (Galatians 1:10).

TVS tells us to pursue fame and popularity. Using the arena of history, Paul Johnson illustrates the futility of the quest for popular relevance: "The study of history moves on, remorselessly, like time itself. Today's sensation becomes tomorrow's irrelevance. The bestseller of one decade becomes the embarrassment of another. The revolutionary theory which convulses the academic world gets cut down in the next age to an ironic footnote" (*A Historian Looks at Jesus*). In contrast, EVS calls us to emulate the servanthood of Christ. It has been well said that everyone ought to fear to die until we have done something that will always live. Since people will go into eternity, our other-centered acts of kindness and sacrificial service that are borne out of the love of Christ will endure forever.

TVS raises wealth and status as a standard of success, security, and identity. But as C. S. Lewis noted in *The Screwtape Letters,* "prosperity knits a man to the World. He feels that he is 'finding his place in it,' while really it is finding its place in him. His increasing reputation, his widening circle of acquaintances, his sense of importance, the growing pressure of absorbing and agreeable work, build up in him a sense of being really at home in earth." EVS elevates the standard of integrity and character. "But you, are you seeking great things for yourself? Do not seek them" (Jeremiah 45:5). God sometimes grants the severe mercy of taking His children's toys away for a time so that they will transfer their hope from the creation to the Creator.

TVS drives us to amass power over people and circumstances; EVS tells us to walk humbly before our God. "Humble yourselves, therefore, under the mighty hand of God, that He may exalt you at the proper time, casting all your anxiety upon Him, because He cares for you" (1 Peter 5:6–7).

But the crucial contrast lies in where these opposing value systems ultimately lead:

TEMPORAL	ETERNAL
Pleasure	Knowing God
Recognition of People	Approval of God
Popularity	Servanthood
Wealth and Status	Integrity and Character
Power	Humility
▼	▼
Emptiness	Fulfillment
Delusion	Reality
Foolishness	Wisdom

People *think* they want pleasure, recognition, popularity, status, and power, but the pursuit of these things, in the final analysis, leads to emptiness, delusion, and foolishness. God has set eternity in our hearts (Ecclesiastes 3:11), and our deepest desires are fulfillment (love, joy, peace), reality (that which does not fade away), and wisdom (skill in living). The only path to this true fulfillment lies in the conscious choice of God's value system over that which is offered by this world. This choice is based on trusting a Person we have not yet seen. "And though you have not seen Him, you love Him, and though you do not see Him now, but believe in Him, you greatly rejoice with joy inexpressible and full of glory, obtaining as the outcome of your faith the salvation of your souls" (1 Peter 1:8–9).

As the story of the wedding at Cana illustrates, the world pours out its best wine first and switches to the cheap wine after people's discernment has been dulled. But our Lord's miracle of turning the water into wine teaches us that for those who follow Him, the best is reserved for last.

YOUR PRESUPPOSITIONS SHAPE YOUR PERSPECTIVE

Part of the problem is that we often fail to review the nonnegotiables to which we claim to be committed. For me, the fundamental presuppositions that form the bedrock of my worldview are, as Francis Schaeffer put it, (1) God is there, and (2) He is not silent. That is, the Author of all creation is a Person who has revealed Himself to humanity in "many portions and in many ways" (Hebrews 1:1), including the general revelation of creation and conscience and the special revelation of dreams, visions, prophets, apostles, and clearest of all, His personal revelation in the Person and work of Jesus Christ. I see the Bible as God's declaration of His character and ways, His love letter to the people He sent His Son to redeem, and His blueprint for how to live life with wisdom, purpose, faith, love, and hope.

Since this is my fundamental presupposition about life, everything should flow out of it. It shapes my perspective on who God is, who we are, where we came from, why we are here, where we are going, and how we should relate to others.

THE IMPLICATIONS OF OUR ASSUMPTIONS

I have discovered that while everyone has a worldview, a philosophy, a set of presuppositions about life that they hold by faith, few people are aware of it. Of the few who can express their fundamental assumptions about human existence, only a fraction have thought through the logical implications of these assumptions. And of this small fraction, only a handful have contrasted these logical implications with the way they actually live. This is one reason why the majority of people can move through life with such a discrepancy between belief and practice.

Moving back to my basic presuppositions that the infinite and personal God exists and has decisively revealed Himself in Christ and the Scriptures, what are the logical implications of such a view? There are several, but the most important is that life is all about God and not about us; all things have been created by Him and for Him (Colossians 1:16), and we exist to serve God and not to persuade God to serve us. In essence, the Bible reminds us again and again that "I am God, and you are not."

Another implication is that since we were created for relationship with the Author of every good thing, we can have no higher purpose than to grow in the knowledge of God, and by His grace and power, to become increasingly like Him.

A third implication is that since the Bible was inspired by the living God, we would be wise to learn, understand, experience, and apply its precepts and principles. The Scriptures reveal that our brief earthly sojourn is designed to prepare us for eternal citizenship in heaven. Thus, it would be the heart of folly to become entangled and enmeshed in that which is "highly esteemed among men" but is "detestable in the sight of God" (Luke 16:15). In our careers, for example, we should execute our tasks with quality and care as servants of Christ rather than pleasers of men (Colossians 3:22–24). Our ambition must be different from that of others; instead of pursuing position, power, prestige, or wealth, we should seek the approval of our God (2 Corinthians 5:9).

A fourth implication is that we can expect to be pulled again and again toward the temporal and away from the eternal, because the truths of Scripture are countercultural. Whenever we are lured away from obedience and service to disobedience and selfishness, it is because we have been deceived into thinking either that we know better than God what is best for us or that God is out of control. Obedience flows out of trust, and we will either obey the devices and desires of our own hearts or the word of Him who made us, loves us, and redeemed us.

Our presuppositions shape our perspective. Our perspective, in turn, shapes our priorities, and our priorities shape our practice.

OUR PERSPECTIVE SHAPES OUR PRIORITIES

Years ago, a minister waited in line to have his car filled with gas just before a long holiday weekend. The attendant worked quickly, but there were many cars ahead of him in front of the service station. Finally, the attendant motioned him toward a vacant pump.

"Reverend," said the young man, "sorry about the delay. It seems as if everyone waits until the last minute to get ready for a long trip." The minister chuckled, "I know what you mean. It's the same in my business."

If ours is an eternal perspective, we will be gripped by the biblical truth that our brief earthly sojourn is designed to prepare us for an eternal heavenly citizenship. The more we align ourselves with this perspective, the more it will have an impact on our short-term and long-term priorities.

My friend Gordon Adams uses the analogy of life as a brief stay in a hotel. In some cases the hotel is a fleabag, and in others, there may be mints on the pillows and flowers on the table. But whatever the hotel's rating, we are still living out of suitcases while we are there. And since we know it is not our home, we don't concern ourselves with changing the decor, even if we dislike the curtains and wallpaper. God never intended room service to replace good home-cooked meals; it is a mistake to confuse hotel life with the glorious dwelling place He is preparing for those who know and love His Son.

Part of our problem is that God's promises seem vague and distant—we have no memories of heaven. But He has given us His word that He will more than make it worth our while. "For here we do not have a lasting city, but we are seeking the city which is to come" (Hebrews 13:14). If we remember that here we are sojourners, strangers, and aliens in exile, our priorities will begin to reflect those of Abraham who "was looking for the city which has foundations, whose architect and builder is God" (Hebrews 11:8–10).

Another friend of mine, Max Anders, recently wrote *The Good Life*, a practical exposition of Paul's epistle to the Ephesians. In it, he draws a sharp contrast between the offerings of the world and those of the Word. While the former touts money, ambition, sex, and clout; the latter promises wealth (Ephesians 1–3), purpose (4:1–5:17), love (5:18–6:9), and true power (6:10–20). Too often, however, our priorities reveal that we are chasing shadows when God offers us real substance.

What will endure in the end? Is there anything we can take with us, or do we leave everything behind? When we travel to another country, we must exchange our currency. The currencies of this world will do us no good in the next unless we previously invested them for Christ's sake in the lives of other people. Other-centered relationships that express the love of Christ are the currency of heaven.

OUR PRIORITIES SHAPE OUR PRACTICE

Listen to the words of someone I had the privilege of meeting on two memorable occasions: "We have a clear sense of birth, but a theoretical sense of death. Understand that you have a certain number of days. There is no good time to die. You don't retire from life and get ready for death. When you leave this planet you will never again have the privilege of sharing the gospel, serving the lost, feeding the poor. This is not a guilt trip, but a reminder to enjoy the opportunity and privilege of representing Christ to the world. This proceeds out of love. The love you give back to Him drives the opportunities you have. We must not just wait to get to heaven, but relish the only opportunities we will have." (June, 1986)

"I am trying to come to grips on a daily basis with what it means to seek first His kingdom. Part of this means not pursuing what our system rewards. There is a problem of drifting back into complacency. God has not promised me tomorrow. There are things to accomplish on this side, and it takes a measure of faith to believe there is something on the other side." (March, 1987)

Mark Pett was suffering from terminal cancer when I took these notes during our conversations. We were the same age, and like I, he was engaged in vocational ministry. Mark gained an extraordinary measure of wisdom through the pain he experienced until he went to be with the Lord in February 1988. He stressed the privilege of practice and the window of opportunity to make a difference during our earthly sojourn.

If our priorities shape our practice, then our practice will reveal our priorities. If our practice does not include such elements as an ongoing renewal of the mind through consistent time in Scripture, a commitment to cultivating growing intimacy with God through prayer, and a sensitivity to the opportunities the Lord gives us to love and serve believers and seekers in our arena of influence, then our priorities are not in alignment with those of Scripture.

There are two one-liners I picked up from my friend Bill Garrison that always challenge me. The first is, "Write your obituary now and see if it will play well in heaven." The second is, "What are you taking under your arm to the ultimate show-and-tell?"

Your presuppositions will shape your perspective, your perspective will shape your priorities, and your priorities will shape your practice. "When you leave this planet you will never again have the privilege of sharing the gospel, serving the lost, feeding the poor."

Disciplined Spirituality

DEPENDENCE AND DISCIPLINE

It is easy to slip into one of two extremes regarding the Christian life. The first extreme overemphasizes our role and minimizes God's role. This position is characterized by the mentality of striving for and living for Jesus. It emphasizes knowledge, rules, rededication efforts, and human activities, and virtually ignores the ministry of the Holy Spirit. The second extreme overemphasizes God's role and minimizes our role. This position is characterized by a "let go and let God" form of passivity. It stresses experience, the supernatural, and the person of the Holy Spirit, and downplays the human side of the coin.

The biblical balance is that the spiritual life is both human *and* divine. Paul places these back to back in Philippians 2:12–13: "So then, my beloved, just as you have always obeyed, not as in my presence only, but now much more in my absence, work out your salvation with fear and trembling; for it is God who is at work in you, both to will and to work for His good pleasure." On the human side, we are responsible to work out (not work for) our salvation, but on the divine side, God is the one who gives us the desire and empowerment to accomplish His purposes.

(Exercise: Read the following passages to see the interrelationship of the human and the divine in the outworking of the Christian life: John 14:15–17; 15:4–11, 26–27; Romans 12:1–8, 17–21; 15:30–32; 1 Corinthians 15:10; 2 Corinthians 2:14; 3:1–6; 6:16–17:1; Galatians 2:20; Ephesians 6:10–20;

Philippians 4:13; Colossians 1:9–12, 28–29; 1 Thessalonians 5:22–24; 2 Thessalonians 2:13–17; Hebrews 4:14–16; 10:19–25; James 4:7–10; 1 Peter 1:22–25; 4:11; 5:6–10; 2 Peter 1:1–11; 1 John 2:3–6.)

Dependence

The life of Christ can only be reproduced in us by the power of the Holy Spirit. As an inner work of God, it is not achieved by human effort, but by divine enabling. Apart from Christ and the power of His Spirit, we can accomplish nothing in the sight of God (John 15:4–5; Acts 1:8). Therefore it is crucial that we develop a conscious sense of dependence upon the Spirit's power in all that we do (see Ephesians 1:19; 3:16; 5:18). "But I say, walk by the Spirit, and you will not carry out the desire of the flesh" (Galatians 5:16). "If we live by the Spirit, let us also walk by the Spirit" (Galatians 5:25). The word for walk in the first verse is general and refers to life in its totality. The word for walk in the second verse is specific and refers to the step-by-step process of daily life. Just as Jesus walked in total dependence upon the life of His Father (John 6:57; 14:10), so we must rest in the same source of power. We were never meant to create life, but to receive and display the life of Christ.

Discipline

Dependence is critical, but there is no growth in the Christian life apart from discipline and self-control. "Discipline yourself for the purpose of godliness" (1 Timothy 4:7). Spirituality is not instantaneous or automatic; it is developed and refined. The epistles are full of commands like believe, obey, walk, present, fight, reckon, hold fast, pursue, draw near, and love. The spiritual life is progressively cultivated in the disciplines of the faith; you and I will not wake up one morning to find ourselves suddenly spiritual. This is why Paul uses the metaphor of an athlete, a soldier, and a farmer to illustrate the discipline of the Christian life (see 1 Corinthians 9:24–27; Ephesians 6:10–18; 2 Timothy 2:3–6). We grow in godliness as we hear and obediently respond to the Word. Spiritual maturity is characterized by the ability to recognize and apply the principles of Scripture to daily experience (Hebrews 5:11–14). The Bible comes alive when its precepts are put into practice, but this does not happen apart from human choice. We must actively choose to have our minds and emotions guided and strengthened by the Holy Spirit.

THE BENEFITS OF THE DISCIPLINES

There has been a resurgence of interest in the classical disciplines of the spiritual life, and in this chapter we will look at the reasons for this recent trend and the benefits of the various disciplines. Although we will focus on the discipline (human responsibility) side of the coin, we must be careful never to lose sight of the dependence (divine sovereignty) side of the coin, since both are equally important.

A number of recent authors have called believers to savor the wealth of the spiritual disciplines that have informed Catholic and Orthodox spirituality for centuries but that have been largely overlooked by Protestants. These authors include Richard J. Foster *(Celebration of Discipline, Freedom of Simplicity, Prayer: Finding the Heart's True Home)*, Dallas Willard *(The Spirit of the Disciplines)*, Henri J. M. Nouwen *(The Way of the Heart)*, Bob Benson Sr. and Michael W. Benson *(Disciplines for the Inner Life)*, Donald S. Whitney *(Spiritual Disciplines for the Christian Life)*, James Earl Massey *(Spiritual Disciplines)*, Siang-Yang Tan and Douglas H. Gregg *(Disciplines of the Holy Spirit)*, and R. Kent Hughes *(Disciplines of a Godly Man)*. All of these writers are united in their view of the spiritual disciplines as crucial means to the pursuit of God. They argue that the classical disciplines of the Christian faith are not optional, but essential practices for those who not only love Jesus, but want to become like Him.

The bulk of Christian churches and denominations pitch their message so low that even if their members actually practiced the spiritual regimens they propose, it is unlikely that they would be distinguishably different from their neighbors. In our Christian subculture, mental assent to doctrine is not directly linked to rigorous pursuit of discipleship. The radical and countercultural biblical message of personal transformation by going for broke to follow Christ has often been reduced to a culture-bound spiritual veneer. Appalled by this, a growing number of leaders in the body of Christ have realized that something more is required of believers than being spectators and head-trippers. They have come to see that nothing less than a serious commitment to engagement in the means of transformation that have been modeled for centuries by Christlike men and women will do. Without a personal commitment to inward change, believers will be dominated, motivated, and manipulated by the cultural network of our society. This is where the historical disciplines of the faith come in.

For many people, the word "discipline" reeks with negative connotations. We often associate it with tyranny, external restraint, legalism, and bondage. But a closer look at Scripture and the lives of the great saints in the history of the faith reveals precisely the opposite. The whole book of Proverbs, for instance, argues that far from limiting our freedom, personal disciplines actually enhance it and give us options we could never have had otherwise. Wisdom is a skill that is developed through instruction and discipline, and this skill in the art of living life with each area under the Lord's dominion frees us to become the people God intended us to be. The pursuit of wisdom, discernment, understanding, and the knowledge of God (see Proverbs 2) requires not only an appetite, but also a willingness to pay the necessary price.

For years, I have desired the ability to sit before the keyboard of a piano and make it ring with glorious music. But my craving to do so has never been matched by a willingness to invest the time, energy, and discipline to make it happen. Only those who pay this price have the freedom to make the instrument sing. Thus, discipline is the pathway to freedom rather than bondage. Like the children's story about the impulsive train who wanted to break loose from the rails and go in its own direction, we may not discover the true "freedom of the rails" until we get bogged down in the earth of our own pursuits in disregard of God's design.

In the New Testament, a quick survey of the gospels through

the lens of discipline reveals that the Lord Jesus engaged in all the classic disciplines such as solitude, silence, simplicity, study, prayer, sacrificial service, and fasting. Jesus understood that these practices were not optional for those who have a passion for the Father's pleasure and honor. Our Lord did not engage in these disciplines as ends in themselves, but as means to know and obey His Father. They moved Him in the direction of the foremost commandment: "You shall love the Lord your God with all your heart and with all your soul and with all your might" (Deuteronomy 6:5; Mark 12:30).

Yet somehow we have bought the illusion that we can be like Christ without imitating His spirituality. Clearly, if we wish to be like our Master, we must imitate His practice; if we believe He knew how to live, we must seek the grace to live like Him. To ask the question "What would Jesus do?" without practicing the habits we already know He practiced is to attempt to run a marathon without prior training. What is evident to us on the physical plane is often obscure to us on the spiritual level. It is clearly absurd to think that we could excel at any sport such as golf or tennis without investing the needed time, training, and practice. But when it comes to living the Christian life, we somehow suppose that we are doing well if we attend church and crack open a Bible once or twice a week. If believers expended the same time and energy in cultivating their spiritual lives as they are willing to invest in becoming reasonably skillful at any sport or hobby, the world would look with wonder at the power of the body of Christ.

We desire to know Christ more deeply, but we shun the lifestyle that would make it happen. By relegating the spiritual to certain times and activities, we are ill-prepared to face the temptations and challenges of daily living in a Christlike way. It is easy to deceive ourselves into thinking that without the active and painful formation of godly character, we will still have the capacity to make the right choices whenever we really need to. But if we have not been exercising and training and practicing behind the scenes, we will not have the skill (wisdom) to perform well when it counts. The disciplines off the stage prepare an actor to perform well when the curtain rises, and the hours of training off the field give an athlete the freedom to play well when the game begins. Similarly, the daily regimen of the spiritual disciplines equips us to live well during the uncertainties and vicissitudes of life. This is what Dallas Willard called the law of indirect preparedness; the disciplines in the background of our lives prepare us for the unexpected times when we will need to respond in appropriate ways. Willpower alone will not be enough, unless our wills have been trained and strengthened through ongoing practice.

There is no shortcut to spiritual formation. After the initial burst of enthusiasm, we soon discover that beginning the process is much easier than following through. As anyone who attempts to learn a new skill quickly realizes, the early learning stages can be particularly challenging, because everything seems no unnatural. Only those who are willing to persevere reach the point where they begin to "get the hang of it." But in the spiritual arena, we never really arrive. Scripture encourages us to continually press on toward the goal and to reach forward to what lies ahead so that we may lay hold of that for which Christ Jesus laid hold of us (Philippians 3:12–14). This requires a lifelong commitment to the disciplines that Jesus, the apostles, and the godly followers of the Way have practiced through the centuries. None of the people whose spiritual vitality we have admired regarded these disciplines as optional, and it would be naive to suppose that we are history's first exceptions.

The disciplines of the faith are never ends in themselves, but means to the end of knowing, loving, and trusting God. As we implement them in a consistent way, we cultivate holy *habits*. As these habits grow, they guide our behavior and character in such a way that it becomes more natural for us to live out our new identities in Christ. Our daily choices shape our habits, and our habits shape our character. Our character, in turn, guides the decisions we make in times of stress, temptation, and adversity. In this way, the godly actions of maturing believers are outward displays of increasing inner beauty.

The spiritual disciplines are the product of a synergy between divine and human initiative, and they serve us as means of grace insofar as they bring the totality of our personalities under the lordship of Christ and the control of the Spirit. By practicing them, we place our minds, temperaments, and bodies before God and seek the grace of His transformation. In this way, we learn to appropriate the power of kingdom living. These disciplines are both active and passive, both initiatory and receptive; they connect us to the power of the indwelling Holy Spirit who manifests the life of Christ in us and through us. Thus, we should work hard, but receive everything we are and have by God's grace. It takes the touch of God on our lives for us to form habits that are alive and pleasing to God.

If we fail to see these disciplines and habits as responses to divine grace, we will slip into the trap of thinking that they have value in themselves. Those who think this way suppose that when they meditate or fast, they are spiritually superior to those who do not. Their disciplines become external, self-energized, and law-driven. They are tempted to quantify spirituality by reducing it to a set of external practices rather than an internal, grace-drawn process of transformation. Instead, we must see the disciplines as external practices that reflect and reinforce internal aspirations. Spiritual growth is inside-out, not outside-in; our focus should be more on the process of inner transformation than on outward routines. This understanding will free us from thinking that the disciplines we practice are magical in themselves or that others should be engaging in the same activities that we practice. Spiritual disciplines are good servants but poor masters; they are useful means but inadequate ends.

To summarize, here are a few of the many benefits of practicing the spiritual disciplines:

1. They encourage the imitation of Christ and allow us to act in ways that are centered in God's will.

2. They personally connect us with an ongoing tradition of time-tested ways of incarnating the spiritual life.

3. They give us a rule of conduct that directs us in the path of growing skill in living before God.

4. They equip us with resources to fight on the battlefronts of the world, the flesh, and the demonic.

5. They confer perspective and power, and they encourage us to embrace God's purpose for our lives.

6. They bestow a controlled freedom to respond to changing circumstances in a more biblical manner; they allow our lives to be dominated more by the things above than the things below.

7. They remind us daily that the spiritual life is a balance between radical dependence and responsible action; both grace and self-discipline are required for spiritual maturity.

8. They are vehicles for internal transformation. Given enough time, an average person who consistently practices spiritual disciplines will achieve spiritual productivity and proficiency.

9. They replace habits of sin by cultivating habits that lead to character (e.g., integrity, faithfulness, and compassion).

10. They increase our willingness to acknowledge the daily cost of discipleship and remind us that whatever comes quickly and cheaply is superficial, while the insights that we learn from pain will endure.

CHAPTER 7

Disciplined Spirituality

WHAT ARE THE
SPIRITUAL DISCIPLINES?

While there is no standardized list of spiritual disciplines, some are more prominent in the literature than others. Richard J. Foster develops a threefold typology of inward disciplines (meditation, prayer, fasting, and study), outward disciplines (simplicity, solitude, submission, and service) and corporate disciplines (confession, worship, guidance, and celebration). Dallas Willard divides the disciplines into two classes: disciplines of abstinence (solitude, silence, fasting, frugality, chastity, secrecy, and sacrifice) and disciplines of engagement (study, worship, celebration, service, prayer, fellowship, confession, and submission). Other writers categorize a variety of other activities as disciplines, including journaling, dialogue, witness, stewardship, and listening.

We will begin with a concise description of twenty of these disciplines. Then using Willard's typology, we will look more closely at two disciplines of abstinence (solitude and silence) and three disciplines of engagement (study, meditation, and prayer). Remember, however, that these disciplines are merely tools to help us grow. It would be a mistake to claim that every follower of Christ should practice all of these disciplines in a consistent or rigorous way. Some will be more essential for you at one time, and some will serve you better at other times. You will find that some of the disciplines are nonnegotiable, while others can be pursued intermittently. Depending on your temperament and circumstances, you will be drawn to some and indifferent to others. Still, it is wise to engage occasionally in the ones you would normally dismiss so that you can experience their unique benefits.

SOLITUDE AND SILENCE

Solitude is the most fundamental of the disciplines in that it moves us away, for a time, from the lures and aspirations of the world into the presence of the Father. In solitude, we remove ourselves from the influence of our peers and society and find the solace of anonymity. In this cloister we discover a place of strength, dependence, reflection, and renewal, and we confront inner patterns and forces that are alien to the life of Christ within us.

Silence is a catalyst of solitude; it prepares the way for inner seclusion and enables us to listen to the quiet voice of the Spirit. Few of us have experienced real silence, and most people would find it to be quite uncomfortable at first. Silence is totally at odds with the din of our culture and the popular addiction to noise and hubbub. This discipline relates not only to finding places of silence in our surroundings, but also times of restricted speech in the presence of others.

PRAYER

Prayer is personal communion and dialogue with the living God. Seen from a biblical perspective, prayer is an opportunity and a privilege rather than a burden or a duty. It is the meeting place where we draw near to God to receive His grace, to release our burdens and fears, and to get honest with the Lord. Prayer should not be limited to structured times, but should also become an ongoing dialogue with God as we practice His presence in the context of our daily activities.

JOURNALING

Many have found that keeping a spiritual diary heightens their understanding of the unique process of spiritual formation through which God has been taking them. By recording our insights, feelings, and the stream of our experiences, we clarify the progress of our spiritual journey. This discipline relates closely to those of prayer, meditation, and study; journaling enhances personal reflection, encourages us to record perspectives we have received from Scripture, and serves as another form of prayer.

STUDY AND MEDITATION

The discipline of study is central to the whole process of renewing the mind in such a way that we can respond in appropriate ways to the truths of God's Word. Study of Scripture involves not only reading, but active involvement in observation, interpretation, and application of its contents. This discipline also includes devotional reflection on the beauties and intricacies of nature as well as exposure to gifted writers and teachers both past and present.

Meditation is a close relative of the disciplines of prayer and study, and it also depends on the disciplines of solitude and silence. Meditation has become such a lost art in the West that we typically associate it with eastern religions. Far from emptying the mind, however, biblical meditation focuses the mind on the nuances of revealed truth. To meditate on the Word is to take the time to ruminate and ponder a verse or a phrase from Scripture so that its truth can become more real and sink more deeply into our being.

FASTING AND CHASTITY

The spiritual discipline of fasting is abstention from physical nourishment for the purpose of spiritual sustenance. This difficult discipline requires practice before it can be effective, since it is not natural for us to pursue self-denial. There are different methods and degrees of fasting, but all of them promote self-control and reveal the degree to which we are ruled by our bodily appetites. Fasting can also consist of abstention from other things that may control us, such as television and other forms of entertainment.

The discipline of chastity is relevant to all believers, whether single or married. This discipline, while recognizing that the sexual appetite is a legitimate part of our nature, encourages us to resist the painful consequences of improper feelings, fantasies, obsessions, and relations that are so frequently reinforced in our culture. Chastity elevates loving concern for the good of others above personal gratification.

SECRECY

The practice of secrecy is dependence on God alone for what should and should not be noticed by others. Secrecy is the opposite of grasping and self-promotion, since it teaches us to love anonymity and frees us from the bondage of the opinions of others. Secrecy is not a false humility, but a heartfelt desire to seek the praise and approval of God regardless of what people may think.

CONFESSION

This discipline sets us free from the burden of hidden sin, but it requires transparency and vulnerability in the presence of one or more people whom we implicitly trust. When we uncover and name our secrets, failures, and weaknesses, they lose their dominion by virtue of being exposed. Sadly, we are generally more concerned about the disapproval of people whom we can see than we are about the disapproval of God whom we cannot see, and this is what makes repentance and confession before others so difficult.

FELLOWSHIP

For some people, the enjoyment of community is not a discipline, but a delight. But there are many in our individualistic culture who are more inclined toward autonomy and independence than to body life. For them, a willingness to actively seek mutual encouragement and edification is a discipline that will eventually pay dividends through regular exposure to a diversity of natural and spiritual gifts.

SUBMISSION AND GUIDANCE

The discipline of voluntary submission to others as an expression of our submission to Christ is based upon the biblical mandate for us to seek the good of others rather than our own rights. Mutual subordination and servanthood frees us from having to be in control and to have things go our own way. By imitating Christ in this discipline of self-denial, we become increasingly concerned with the needs of others.

The discipline of guidance involves the recovery of the widely overlooked pursuit of spiritual direction. In recent years, there has been a growing awareness in the evangelical community of the need for seeking spiritual guidance through accountability to mentors whose credibility is established by experience and maturity. Guidance is also a corporate discipline in which a body of believers seeks a Spirit-directed unity.

SIMPLICITY, STEWARDSHIP, AND SACRIFICE

These disciplines reinforce each other since they all relate to our attitude and to the use of the resources that have been placed at our disposal. The discipline of simplicity or frugality refers to a willingness to abstain from the use of these resources for our own gratification and aggrandizement. A mind-set of simplicity helps us resist the cultural endorsement of extravagance and consumption that entices us away from gratitude, trust, and dependence upon the Lord. This discipline frees us from the multiplicity of fleshly desires and anxiety over trivial things, and it helps to deliver us from the bondage of financial debt.

The related discipline of stewardship encourages us to reflect on our lives as managers of the assets of Another. In addition to the usual trilogy of *time, talent,* and *treasure,* I also include the stewardship of the *truth* we have received as well as the *relationships* with which we have been entrusted. In this discipline, we periodically review the ways we have been investing these assets.

Sacrifice is a more radical discipline than simplicity in that it involves the occasional risk of giving up something we would use to meet our needs rather than our wants. This is a faith-building exercise that commits us to entrust ourselves to God's care.

WORSHIP AND CELEBRATION

To worship is to be fully occupied with the attributes of God—the majesty, beauty, and goodness of His person, powers, and perfections. For the individual, worship often involves devotional reflection on the person and work of Jesus Christ as our mediator to the Father. In a corporate setting, believers are united together in heart and mind to honor and extol the infinite and personal God. The discipline of worship expands our concept of who God is and what He has done.

Celebration focuses on all that God has done on our behalf. It is the discipline of choosing gratitude rather than grumbling and remembrance rather than indifference. When we celebrate, we review and relive the history of God's blessings, and this stimulates a renewed sense of devotion. Celebration, whether individual or corporate, is taking pleasure, amazement, and joy in how good God has been to us in specific ways and times. To revel in God's goodness is to gain a new sense of perspective.

SERVICE

The discipline of service does not call attention to itself but to the needs and concerns of others. True service does not look for recognition but is borne out of love for Jesus and a desire to follow Him in "washing the feet" of the saints. In this discipline, we take on roles that are passed over and that do not call attention to ourselves; we steadfastly refuse to live for appearance and recognition, choosing instead to show kindness, courtesy, sensitivity, and concern for people who are often overlooked.

WITNESS

The reason many believers are not involved in evangelism is that they do not see it as a discipline that requires a corresponding lifestyle. To witness is to choose to go beyond our circle of believing friends and to walk dependently in the power of the Spirit as we invest in relationships with those who have not yet met Christ. The discipline of witness takes seriously the biblical mandate of bearing witness to Jesus by building nonmanipulative relationships with eternity in view.

THE DISCIPLINE OF SOLITUDE

Although many believers, especially extroverts, completely avoid this primary discipline of the faith, the spiritual cost in doing so is simply too great. Even a casual look at the gospels reveals that solitude was an indispensable practice in the life of the Lord Jesus (see Matthew 14:23; Mark 1:35; Luke 5:16; John 6:15) as it was in the lives of all the great saints who have preceded us. It was in the solitude of the wilderness that Jesus prepared to inaugurate His public ministry (Matthew 4:1–11); it was in the solitude of the mountain that He prepared to select His disciples (Luke 6:12); and it was in the solitude of the garden that He prepared to sacrifice His life for the sins of the world (Matthew 26:36–46). Solitude transcends loneliness—whenever Jesus sought solitude, it was to be in the presence of His Father. Solitude also transcends place, since Jesus practiced an inner solitude of heart and mind even when He was in the midst of people.

It is in solitude that we remove ourselves from the siren calls and illusions of our society and wrestle with the need for ongoing transformation as we meet with the Lord. Dietrich Bonhoeffer in *Life Together* warned: "Let him who cannot be alone beware of community.... Let him who is not in community beware of being alone." Times deliberately spent away from interaction with other people nurture depth, perspective, purpose, and resolve. They deliver us from the tyranny and distractions of daily routine and prepare us for the next stage of the journey through an inner call rather than an external compulsion. By periodically distancing ourselves from schedules, noise, and crowds, we become less captivated by the demands and expectations of others and more captivated by the purposes of God. In this way, we measure and define ourselves in terms of what God thinks rather than what people think. This, in turn, empowers us to serve and show compassion to others, since we are less manipulated by human expectations and more alive to divine intentions.

Extended times spent in solitude can be frightening, since they remove our external props and force us to confront sinful and selfish attitudes and behaviors. Such times can make us uncomfortably vulnerable before God, but this is as it should be, since this process drives us to the grace, forgiveness, and love of Christ. The purgation of solitude diminishes arrogance and autonomy and fosters humility and trust. As this discipline moves us in the direction of greater Christlikeness, ministry to others becomes an extension of our being.

It is good to have a place for daily meeting alone with the Lord. But we can also carry an inner spirit of solitude with us even in the presence of others. Each day is also clustered with opportunities for little moments of solitude (e.g., driving alone) if we come to see them in this way.

More extended seasons of solitude can be pivotal in our growth, but they require planning and resolve. I periodically plan a one-day personal retreat for solitude, silence, prayer, and reflection at a friend's cabin in the country. I have always profited from these retreats, but they never happen unless I put them in my calendar far in advance. Even then, I am tempted to find a dozen excuses for not going when the time arrives. This is where the discipline of choice over feelings comes in.

THE DISCIPLINE OF SILENCE

Solitude and silence are companion disciplines; silence gives depth to solitude, and solitude creates a place for silence. Similarly, both of these disciplines can be practiced inwardly (whether we are with people or not) as well as outwardly.

"Where shall the world be found, where will the word resound? Not here, there is not enough silence." When T. S. Eliot wrote these words, he succinctly captured the essence of our zeitgeist, the spirit of our time and culture. The contemporary epidemic of drivenness to crowds, words, music, entertainment, and noise is inimical to the life of the spirit and points to an inner emptiness. I am convinced that many people would begin to experience withdrawal symptoms if they were completely deprived of these sounds for more than an hour. Only a minority of us even know what total silence is like.

"In repentance and rest you shall be saved, in quietness and trust is your strength" (Isaiah 30:15). The transformational discipline of silence encourages us to grow "in quietness and trust" by being still and hushed before God so that we can listen with our spirit to Him and enjoy His presence. This discipline also extends to our relationships with people. Silence in the presence of others can be practiced by deliberately speaking less than we otherwise would in a number of situations. James encourages us to turn this practice into a lifestyle: "Let everyone must be quick to hear, slow to speak and slow to anger" (James 1:19; also see 1:26; 3:2–12). Solomon added, "When there are many words, transgression is unavoidable, but he who restrains his lips is wise" (Proverbs 10:19). Consider how much less people would say if they eliminated boasting (Proverbs 25:14; 27:1–2), gossip and slander (Proverbs 11:13; 18:8; 20:19), flattery (Proverbs 26:28; 29:5), nagging (Proverbs 19:13; 21:9, 19; 27:15–16), and quarreling (Proverbs 20:3; 26:21; 2 Timothy 2:23–24) from their speech! Although words can have healing and life-giving power, there are far more occasions when I have regretted opening my mouth than I have regretted remaining silent. Like toothpaste, once the words are out, we cannot put them back in the tube by unsaying them. The discipline of silence increases our psychic margin by giving us the time and composure to weigh our words carefully and use them in more appropriate ways. Silence not only increases our poise and credibility, but it also enables us to be better observers and more effective, other-centered listeners. In addition, this discipline makes us less inclined to use words to control people or manipulate them into approving and affirming us.

Although many have observed that it is easier to be completely silent than to speak in moderation, it would be well worth spending a day in unbroken silence. (If you try this, it goes without saying that you should previously inform others of your intention.) Such a verbal fast would be a real source of illumination about our social strategies and devices.

Henri Nouwen observed that silence "can be seen as a portable cell taken with us from the solitary place into the midst of our ministry." Clearly, the discipline of silence before God and people relates to the practice of self-control; the more we develop inner control and composure, the less we will feel compelled to gain outward control over people and circumstances.

THE DISCIPLINE OF STUDY

Since the study of Scripture is the primary vehicle for laying hold of a divine perspective on the world and our purpose in it, this discipline is pivotal to our spiritual nourishment and growth (2 Timothy 3:16–17). Consistent study of the Word cultivates eternal values and priorities, provides guidance for decision making, assists us in overcoming temptation, and enhances our knowledge of God and of ourselves.

The problem is that most people are daunted by the prospect of personal Bible study, since they have little idea of what to do. The hit-and-miss approach of Bible roulette provides little spiritual nourishment. Without an ability to understand and apply the truths of Scripture in a practical and meaningful way, believers miss out on the benefits of exploring and discovering biblical truths for themselves. This is why so many Christians have only a secondhand knowledge of the Bible and rely almost exclusively on the input of teachers and preachers.

There are many helpful resources that offer useful methods and can guide you through the process of effective Bible study. But here are a few principles and suggestions that may help:

- ♦ Maintain a posture of openness and honesty before the Word so that you will be disposed to gain new insights and change your thinking. Be responsive to what you read and study and be willing to apply and obey what you learn. Remember that you are engaging in this discipline to meet God and know Him better.
- ♦ Avail yourself of the whole counsel of Scripture (the historical, poetical, and prophetical books as well as the gospels and epistles).
- ♦ Try to be consistent in your exposure to Scripture; this will often require the choice to study whether you feel like it or not.

♦ Do not regard the Bible as a textbook; it is not merely an object to be observed but an oracle to be obeyed. Approach it with a proper attitude of reverence, care, and receptivity.

♦ Try to be systematic in your choice of topics, chapters, and books that you study so that your input will come from all parts of Scripture and touch upon every aspect of your life.

♦ Ask, answer, accumulate, and apply. *Ask* key questions that when answered will provide insight into the meaning of the passage. Use the text (immediate and broad context) as well as standard tools (a concordance, Bible dictionary or encyclopedia, or a Bible commentary) to *answer* your questions. *Accumulate* practical principles such as promises to claim, commands to obey, or sins to confess. *Apply* these principles to your life and relationships.

♦ Have a plan for daily Bible readings so that you will get a comprehensive exposure to Scripture. Reflect on your readings and respond to them in a personal way.

♦ Use a card to write down key passages that speak to you and carry one or more of these cards with you. By reviewing these cards from time to time, you can memorize a significant number of verses. The verses you memorize will be of great benefit to you, especially in times of temptation and trials.

♦ Try studying a whole book of Scripture either synthetically or analytically. In the *synthetic method,* you seek a comprehensive picture that will help you see how the pieces of the puzzle fit together. Start with a short book and read it several times. Record the principles you find and create a title for each paragraph in the book. Finally, write a paragraph to summarize the main theme of the book. Show how each of the book's paragraphs contributes to the development of this theme. In the *analytical method,* you focus on the details and particulars of a passage and employ a more in-depth analysis of the Word. Start with a single paragraph and read it several times. As you read and reflect on your paragraph, engage in observation, interpretation, correlation, and application. In *observation,* you ask basic questions of the text, look for key words, phrases, and verses, find connecting words and progressions of thought, and discover contrasts and comparisons. In *interpretation,* you seek to understand the things you have observed to discern the meaning and purpose that the author had in mind. In *correlation,* you relate the passage you are studying to the overall context and coordinate it with other sections of Scripture. In *application,* you derive specific principles from what you have learned and seek to implement them in your life.

♦ The *topical method* of Bible study helps you discover the development of a theme through the pages of Scripture. Choose a specific topic and decide whether you wish to trace it from Genesis to Revelation or limit yourself to its use in a section or book of the Bible or in a series of selected verses. You may want to choose a theme like sin, redemption, forgiveness, love, or wisdom. Or you may study a concept like speech, the family, stewardship, or work. Use a concordance (*Nave's Topical Bible* is also helpful) to find the passages you will work with. Make your observations, ask questions, look for the answers, and then formulate an outline of the topic to organize your key thoughts. Check and supplement your results by using a Bible encyclopedia. Summarize your findings and be sure to end with a set of specific life applications.

♦ The *biographical method* involves a study of the failures and successes of Bible personalities. This is an excellent way to uncover spiritual principles and discover insights into the way God works in people's lives. If the person you want to study is a major figure in Scripture, you may want to confine your study to a particular book or a portion of his or her life. Use a concordance to find the relevant passages. As you work with these verses, create a list of the events in the person's life and then arrange them in a chronological sequence. Use this list to develop a biographical outline with the associated verses. With this outline, move through

the character's life and make a set of observations, inter-
pretations, and applications.

The discipline of study is not limited to the Bible, but extends
to exposure to the classics of the faith (St. Augustine, *Confessions;*
Bernard of Clairvaux, *On the Love of God;* Thomas à Kempis, *The
Imitation of Christ;* John Calvin, *Institutes of the Christian Religion;*
St. Francis de Sales, *Introduction to the Devout Life;* Blaise Pascal,
Pensées; John Bunyan, *Pilgrim's Progress;* François Fénelon,
Christian Perfection; William Law, *A Serious Call to a Devout and
Holy Life,* to name just a few) as well as more contemporary writ-
ers and teachers. Study can also relate to a growing knowledge and
appreciation of the wonders of creation as well as an awareness of
the benefits and dangers of our culture.

It is well to sustain an attitude of humility and teachability so
that you will always have the mind-set of a learner. In this way, you
will remain fresh and alive to new perspectives and insights and
resist the encroaching disease of "hardening of the categories."

THE DISCIPLINE OF MEDITATION

It is impossible to think about nothing. Try it, and you will be
aware of yourself trying to be aware of nothing—a zoo of images
and thoughts will run through your mind in spite of your efforts
to squelch them. When you ask someone what she is thinking
about and she responds, "Oh, nothing," you know this cannot be
so. Since the mind does not shut off, the issue is not whether we
will think or even meditate; it is what we will think about and
where we will direct our thoughts.

Listen to this old proverb:

Sow a thought, reap an act;
Sow an act, reap a habit;
Sow a habit, reap a character;
Sow a character, reap a destiny.

Whether we like it or not, we are always sowing thoughts, since
our minds are constantly dwelling on something. The experience of

discursive meditation is universal, but the practice of directed meditation is rare. The discipline comes in the effort to deliberately choose that upon which we will set our minds and in the skill of gently returning to it when we find that we have wandered.

As the saints in previous centuries have attested, meditation is an integral component of Christian spirituality, and yet it has largely fallen into disuse in our time. Many believers have become suspicious of the whole idea, since they think it refers only to the consciousness-voiding techniques of Buddhism, Hinduism, and the New Age movement. But as the psalms make clear, a biblical approach to meditation does not empty one's consciousness, but fills it with the truths of God's revealed Word. To meditate on Scripture and on the person and works of God is to take nourishment for our souls by extending our roots more deeply into holy ground. The more we take root downward, the more we will bear fruit upward (Isaiah 37:31). As we feed on the Lord by focusing our minds, affections, and wills on Him and on His words (Joshua 1:8; Psalm 1:2–3; John 6:63), we commune with Him and manifest the fruit of abiding in Him (John 15:4–8).

The apostle Paul underscored the importance of the believer's thought life when he encouraged the Romans to set their minds on the things of the Spirit and not on the things of the flesh (Romans 8:4–9), and when he instructed the Colossians to set their minds on the things above, not on the things that are on earth (Colossians 3:1–2). Similarly, he exhorted the Philippians to engage in a biblical form of positive thinking: "Finally, brethren, whatever is true, whatever is honorable, whatever is right, whatever is pure, whatever is lovely, whatever is of good repute, if there is any excellence and if anything worthy of praise, dwell on these things" (Philippians 4:8). This is not an easy practice, since it is far easier to dwell on thoughts that are untrue, dishonorable, wrong, impure, and ugly, and on things that are of bad repute, shoddy, and worthy of blame. Gossip and criticism are often more appealing in conversation about others than commendation and praise. In addition, we are more likely to view our circumstances in terms of the benefits we lack rather than the blessings we have received, and this is why our' prayers are high on petition and low on thanksgiving. (If you don't believe this, try offering nothing but prayers of thanksgiving for twenty minutes, and see how often you have the impulse to slip in prayers of request!) Remember that the heart will make room for that upon which it dwells.

Here are some suggestions to assist you in this life-giving discipline:

- ♦ Choose very brief passages from Scripture that are meaningful to you. One or two verses can become the theme of one day's meditation.
- ♦ Select specific times for brief interludes of meditation on the text you have chosen for the day. These could be before meals and coffee breaks, or you could use a watch with an alarm to remind you at regular intervals throughout the day (when the alarm sounds, immediately set it for the next brief meditation break).
- ♦ Use your imagination and begin to visualize the concepts in the text in as many ways as you can. Put yourself into the words and into the historical context of the verse.
- ♦ Ponder each word and phrase of the text and try to gain as many insights as you can. Creatively approach it from different angles, and ask the Spirit of God to minister to you through this process.
- ♦ Personalize the passage and make it your own by putting it in the first person and praying it back to God. Commit yourself to pursue and apply the truths you have found in it.
- ♦ Offer praise and worship to God on the basis of your day's meditation.
- ♦ Jim Downing in his book on meditation suggests a plan that involves the daily reading of every thirtieth psalm, starting with the psalm that corresponds by number to the day of the month. Five minutes before going to bed, read through the next day's psalms until you find a verse that particularly speaks to you. Then close your Bible and be sure to make that your last waking thought. If you wake up

during the night, think about the verse. In the morning, read through the five psalms with your verse in mind and let it be the theme of your meditation that day.

♦ Meditation directs the conscious mind during the day, and is an excellent way to practice the presence of God. The H.W.L.W. habit—His Word the Last Word before retiring—programs the subconscious mind during the night (Psalm 63:6; Proverbs 6:22).

♦ The only way you will develop skill in meditation is by doing it, even when it does not seem to be effective.

THE DISCIPLINE OF PRAYER

The concept of communicating with God, talking directly and openly with Him just as we would talk with an intimate friend, is one of the great truths of Scripture. As John Piper observed in *The Pleasures of God,* "Prayer is God's delight because it shows the reaches of our poverty and the riches of His grace." When prayer is overlooked or appended as an afterthought to service, the power of God is often absent. It is dangerously easy to move away from dependence upon God and to slip into the trap of self-reliance. But prayer and action are complementary, not contradictory, and it is wise to overlap them as much as possible. Christian service is most effective when prayer not only precedes it but also flows together with it.

Why Should We Pray?

There are many reasons for making this discipline the centerpiece of your spiritual journey. Here are ten:

1. Prayer enhances our fellowship and intimacy with God (Psalm 116:1–2; Jeremiah 33:2–3).

2. The Scriptures command us to pray (Luke 18:1; Ephesians 6:18; 1 Thessalonians 5:16–18; 1 Timothy 2:1).

3. When we pray, we follow the example of Christ and other great people in Scripture like Moses and Elijah (Mark 1:35; Numbers 11:2; 1 Kings 18:36–37).

4. Prayer appropriates God's power for our lives (John 15:5;

Acts 4:31; Ephesians 3:16; Colossians 4:2–4).

5. We receive special help from God when we pray (Hebrews 4:16).

6. Prayer makes a genuine difference (Luke 11:9–10; James 5:16–18). As William Temple observed, "When I pray, coincidences happen; when I don't, they don't."

7. Prayer develops our understanding and knowledge of God (Psalm 37:3–6; 63:1–8; Ephesians 1:16–19).

8. Our prayers and God's answers give us joy and peace in our hearts (John 16:23–24; Philippians 4:6–7). Our problems may not disappear, but in prayer we gain a new perspective on our problems along with the peace and patience to stand firm.

9. Prayer helps us understand and accomplish God's purposes for our lives (Colossians 1:9–11).

10. Prayer changes our attitudes and desires (2 Corinthians 12:7–9).

Suggestions for Enhancing Your Practice of Prayer
Choose the best time. Select a particular time of the day and dedicate it to personal prayer only. For most of us, the morning is best because we have been refreshed by the previous night's rest, and we are not yet absorbed in the demands of the day. This is often the time we can keep most consistently, and during morning prayer we can dedicate the day to the Lord. It is extremely wise to bring Him into our decision-making process by thinking through and planning the day's activities in prayer. "If God is not first in our thoughts and efforts in the morning, he will be in the last place the remainder of the day" (E. M. Bounds).

Choose the best place. Select a place where there will be a minimum of interruptions and distractions. If possible, pray away from your phone and your desk. When the weather and your schedule permit, you may want to try praying during a walk.

Set a minimum time for daily prayer. Try to be realistic—don't attempt too much at first or your prayer life will become mechanical and discouraging. Start with a few minutes and gradually build from there. Faithfulness on this level will lead to an increased appetite and you will actually look forward to the times you spend with God. "In prayer, quality is always better than quantity" (Robert Coleman). Nevertheless, quality should not become a substitute for quantity. "Surely the experience of all good men confirms the proposition that without a due measure of private devotions the soul will grow lean" (William Wilberforce).

Be consistent. Regard your prayer time as a daily appointment you have made with God and respect it as such. If the discipline of regular time with God is not a matter of the highest priority, your spiritual life will suffer, and this will ultimately affect every other aspect of your life. Set your heart to pursue the person, knowledge, and ways of God by spending regular time with Him.

Focus on the person of God. Prepare your heart and mind for prayer by releasing all stresses and concerns and giving them to the Lord. It is a good practice to read or meditate upon a passage of Scripture and then to concentrate your attention on the presence of Christ in your life. Rest in His presence, "casting all your anxiety upon Him, because He cares for you" (1 Peter 5:7).

Come before Him in humility. You are in the unmediated presence of the holy God who is like a blazing light and a consuming fire, before whom all things are manifest. Judge yourself to be sure that you are approaching Him in honesty and openness, with no barriers of unconfessed sin, because He hates sin and cover-ups. Sometimes we get too casual before the One who spoke the hundreds of billions of galaxies into existence.

Come expectantly to the throne. The significance of prayer is not what we are asking, but the Person we are addressing. Come in simplicity and trust like a child to a father. Expect the supernatural—ask Him for something only He could do ("Is anything too difficult for the LORD?" Genesis 18:14) and watch what happens.

Pray at all times in the Spirit. "We do not know how to pray as we should, but the Spirit Himself intercedes for us with groanings too deep for words" (Romans 8:26). Our prayers should be initiated and energized by the Holy Spirit who "intercedes for the saints according to the will of God" (Romans 8:27).

Strive for a balanced diet. Our prayers should incorporate all the elements of confession, adoration, supplication (intercession and petition), and thanksgiving. We are usually short on adoration and thanksgiving.

Pray Scripture back to God. By personalizing passages of Scripture and offering them back to the Lord, you integrate them in your own life and experience and think God's thoughts after Him.

Do not do all the talking. Practice times of silence before the Lord so that you can be sensitive to the promptings of His Spirit. Be responsive to Him by confessing any areas of exposed sin, interceding for others, praying for wisdom, and submitting to His desires.

Make prayer a part of your relationships with people. Personal prayer is crucial, but it must not crowd out corporate prayer. Prayer should be a part of the home and part of Christian friendships. Great benefit can be derived from setting up a prayer partnership with another person, a prayer cell with a few people, or a prayer fellowship with several people.

Plan special times of prayer during the year. You may want to consider setting aside one or more special times (a morning or evening or a whole day) for a personal or small group prayer retreat. This can be especially meaningful when done in the context of planning ahead for the next several months or when a critical decision must be made.

Practice the presence of God. Helmut Thielicke noted that "prayer is no longer the active soil of our life, our home, the air we breathe." When ministry becomes a substitute for prayer, it becomes self-dependent and ineffective. We should desire not only to have one or more times that are formally dedicated to prayer during the day, but also to be conscious of the presence of God throughout the day. In this way, each task is rendered in His name and done in conscious dependence upon Him. Another desirable habit we should seek to cultivate is to pray for others as we see them and talk with them. This can radically affect our attitudes and behavior. A third beneficial habit is to begin to associate our work with prayer. "It is not prayer in addition to work, but prayer simultaneous with work. We precede, enfold, and follow all our work with prayer. Prayer and action become wedded" (Richard Foster).

Lectio Divina

The ancient art of *lectio divina,* or sacred reading, was introduced to the West by the Eastern desert father John Cassian early in the fifth century. It has been practiced for centuries by Cistercian monks (e.g., Michael Casey, *Sacred Reading* and *Toward God)* and is now being rediscovered in wider parts of the Christian community. This extraordinarily beneficial approach combines the disciplines of study, prayer, and meditation into a powerful method that when consistently applied, can revolutionize one's spiritual life. Sacred reading consists of four elements:

1. *Lectio* (reading). Select a very short text and ingest it by reading it several times. I normally choose a verse or two from the chapters I read from the Old and New Testaments in my morning Bible reading.

2. *Meditatio* (meditation). Take a few minutes to reflect and ruminate over the words and phrases in the text you have read. Ponder the passage by asking questions and using your imagination.

3. *Oratio* (prayer). Having internalized the passage, offer it back to God in the form of personalized prayer.

4. *Contemplatio* (contemplation). For most of us, this will be the most difficult part, since it consists of silence and yieldedness in the presence of God. Contemplation is the fruit of the dialogue of the first three elements; it is the communion that is borne out of our reception of divine truth in our minds and hearts.

In spite of a multitude of inner distractions and times when God seems silent, practice and perseverance in *lectio divina* is profoundly rewarding.

CHAPTER 8

Exchanged Life Spirituality

GRASPING OUR TRUE
IDENTITY IN CHRIST

The last century has seen the growth of an experiential approach to the spiritual life that is based on the believer's new identity in Christ. Identification with Christ in His crucifixion and resurrection (Romans 6; Galatians 2:20) means that our old life has been exchanged for the life of Christ. This approach to spirituality moves from a works to a grace orientation and from legalism to liberty because it centers on our acknowledgment that Christ's life is our life.

When I was in seminary, I took a memorable course taught by Howard Hendricks on the spiritual life. In the first half of the course, he constructed a series of contrasts and emphasized that the spiritual life is *not:*

+ a crisis, but a continual process.
+ based on knowledge, but on obedience.
+ external, but internal.
+ automatic, but cultivated.
+ the product of energy, but of divine enablement.
+ a dream, but a discipline.
+ an unusual experience, but a normal experience.
+ a list of rules, but a life relationship.
+ to be endured, but enjoyed.
+ theoretical, but intensely practical.

In the second half of the course, Hendricks defined and developed the spiritual life as "the life of Christ reproduced in the believer by the power of the Holy Spirit in obedient response to the Word of God." The personal and experiential apprehension of "the life of Christ reproduced in the believer by the power of the Holy Spirit" is central to what writers like Hudson Taylor, F. B. Meyer, and Charles Solomon have called the exchanged life. Others have called it the abiding life (Andrew Murray), the victorious life (Charles Trumbull and Bill Gillham), the highest life (Oswald Chambers), life on the highest plane (Ruth Paxon), the normal Christian life (Watchman Nee), the fullness of Christ (Stuart Briscoe), the saving life of Christ (Ian Thomas), the overflowing life (F. R. Havergal), the Christian's secret to a happy life (Hannah Whitall Smith), the larger life (A. B. Simpson), and victory over the darkness (Neil T. Anderson), to name a few.

Exchanged life spirituality concentrates on the reality of an entirely new identity through the in-Christ relationship that can dramatically transform us as we progressively grasp it in our experience.

People without a relationship with their personal Creator are hungering for love, happiness, meaning, and fulfillment, but nothing that this planet offers can fully satisfy these longings. In theory, Christians acknowledge that God alone can meet these needs; but in practice, many believers hardly differ from unbelievers in the ways they try to get them met. This is because they have missed one of the most important principles of Scripture: love, joy, and peace cannot be obtained by pursuing these things as ends in themselves; *they are the overflow and the by-product of the pursuit of God.*

Moses prayed in the wilderness, "Let me know Thy ways, that I may know Thee, so that I may find favor in Thy sight" and God responded, "My presence shall go with you, and I will give you rest" (Exodus 33:13–14). Like Moses, our prayer should be to know God and His ways. By putting Him first, everything else falls into place.

GOD'S CHARACTER AND PLAN

In our quest for greater knowledge and spiritual growth, we sometimes overlook or forget the foundational truths of the faith. Unless we remember to return and build upon the basic biblical doctrines, our spiritual progress will be stifled. The most basic of all these truths is the character of God, and it is in this holy ground that the Christian life is rooted.

God's character is fundamental to everything else. In Scripture, He has revealed His *person, powers,* and *perfections.* In His *person,* He is the self-existent, infinite, eternal, and unchanging Creator of all things. In His *powers,* He alone is omnipresent, omnipotent, and omniscient. In His *perfections,* His attributes include holiness, justice, truthfulness, love, and goodness. We cannot hope to understand the spiritual life unless we lay hold of and cling to the truth of God's character, especially His love and goodness.

God's *love* is manifested in the fact that He is a giver. From the very beginning, He has given in spite of the fact that people have rejected His gifts more often than they have received them. The essence of love is to give and to seek the highest good of the recipient.

> For God so loved the world, that He gave His only begotten Son, that whoever believes in Him should not perish, but have eternal life. (John 3:16)
>
> Husbands, love your wives, just as Christ also loved the church and gave Himself up for her. (Ephesians 5:25)

If we want to understand what God has done for us, we must believe that all His actions are borne out of love. When God loves, He is simply being Himself (1 John 4:8).

God's *goodness* is manifested in His plan of bringing salvation upon the earth and in His ultimate intention for humanity. It is His desire in the ages to come to "show the surpassing riches of His grace in kindness toward us in Christ Jesus" (Ephesians 2:7). He wants to be kind to us forever and He is committed to our joy.

God always acts for our benefit—He is the initiator of redemption, blessings, beauty, and purpose in life. Scripture portrays the relationship He wants with us in terms of a shepherd and his sheep, a father and his children, and a husband and his wife.

However, sheep can go astray, children can rebel, and a wife can be unfaithful. It is this rebellion and rejection of God's love and goodness that has led to the problem of evil and suffering. All of us live in a world of pain, injustice, disease, and death, and in the midst of this it is easy to blame God for our problems. But our environment has been distorted by sin, and sin is that which is contrary to the character of God. Christ entered into our environment of natural and moral evil in order to overcome sin and death. "For God did not send the Son into the world to judge the world, but that the world should be saved through Him" (John 3:17). If we want to understand God and His goodness, we must cling to His character in the face of life's pain:

> The LORD is gracious and merciful; slow to anger and great in lovingkindness.
> The LORD is good to all, and His mercies are over all His works. (Psalm 145:8–9)

The better we grasp the love and goodness of God's character, the less we will be tempted to think that He is carrying out His plans at our expense. It is always to our advantage to conform to His will, because it leads to our highest good. Obedience to God produces joy and fulfillment; disobedience produces sorrow and frustration. There is greater pain in disobedience than in faithfulness. Everything God asks of us is for our good; everything He asks us to avoid is harmful. This is what Evelyn Underhill calls "the sanity of holiness."

Because of who He is, God can be trusted. His plan reflects His character. This plan involved innocent creatures created in His image who would continue to develop physically, intellectually, emotionally, and spiritually in such a way that they would glorify God by becoming more like Him and displaying to the entire universe the beauty of His handiwork. The physical and the spiritual were perfectly integrated, and God's people were to enjoy unimpeded fellowship with Him and each other.

But love always involves a choice, and God's loving and good purpose was distorted by human rebellion. Faced with the decision of whether to abide in God's life or try to create lives of their own, the man and the woman sought to establish themselves as the base for their own meaning. Thus they became sinners by nature and antithetical to the character of God. Beauty was replaced by ugliness, holiness with evil, kindness with cruelty, generosity with greed, love with hate, peace with violence, security with fear, and joy with anger. The Adamic inheritance of physical and spiritual death has been passed from generation to generation, and no one is untainted by sin.

Left to ourselves, we are completely unable to fulfill the purpose for which we have been created. But God has not left us to ourselves—with the Fall, He immediately began to put a plan into effect which would restore humanity to His ultimate intention. God is not only our Creator but also our Redeemer; in Christ, He has made it possible for us to be given a completely new heredity. By removing us out of the line of Adam and placing us in the line of Christ, He has once again placed us in a position where we will ultimately show forth His glory in our spirits, souls, and bodies. In this way, He will demonstrate through us to all creation that He is who He says He is.

Our Old and New Natures

Prior to the Fall, people were in complete harmony with God and with their environment. In their innocence, they were alive to God in their spirits and enjoyed daily and direct communion with Him. This fellowship was reflected in their growing and expanding minds, emotions, and wills. Their bodies were flawlessly adapted to the perfect world in which they lived; they were fully suited to the exquisite creation around them.

But because of their rebellion against God, both humans and their world were radically changed. They suffered spiritual death in that their spirits were cut off from God.

When their spirits died, their sin nature was born, and their minds, emotions, and wills came under the dominion of sin with all its distorting effects. Their bodies also began to deteriorate; physical maladies and death became harsh realities. Pain and evil spread, and the creation itself was corrupted (Romans 8:20–22).

Fallen people sin because they are sinful by nature. It is not that they are sinners because they commit certain sins. Without the redemptive work of Christ, we would be cut off from God without hope of restoration, because "those who are in the flesh cannot please God" (Romans 8:8). But in His love and goodness, God has provided a way to deliver us from this slavery to sin and death. When people place their trust in Christ, they become new creatures (2 Corinthians 5:17) with spirits that are fully in tune with God. "And if Christ is in you, though the body is dead because of sin, yet the spirit is alive because of righteousness" (Romans 8:10). The believer's new self is in the likeness of God and has been "created in righteousness and holiness of the truth" (Ephesians 4:24).

Unlike those who are fallen, those who are redeemed are able not to sin. As they walk in the Spirit, they please God and exhibit Christlikeness. But there is warfare in the Christian's life between the inner self and the outer self. The inner self joyfully concurs with the law of God (Romans 7:22), but there is still a law or power of sin in the outer self (Romans 7:23). Our deepest identity as spiritual beings has been transformed, but our redemption is not yet complete. We still await the "the redemption of our body" (Romans 8:23) when we will be brought into conformity with the glory of Christ's resurrected body (Philippians 3:21). Then the inner and the outer will be perfectly integrated; we will be completely free from the power of sin, and our minds, emotions, and wills will continually be under the dominion of the Spirit of God. Until that time comes, we have been called to the task of allowing God to gradually conform our outer selves to the righteousness and holiness which was created in our inner selves at the moment of salvation. We cannot consistently behave in ways that are different from what we believe about ourselves. A battle rages, but we must realize that the warfare is between the real people we have become in Christ and the mortal remnants of the old people we were in Adam (Romans 5:12–21).

OUR GOD-CREATED NEEDS

This conflict in the believer's life between the inner self and the outer self, this warfare between the spirit and the flesh, is most clearly evident in the territory of our physical and psychological needs and the course we take to fulfill them. These needs are legitimate and God-implanted, and it is His intention to satisfy them and thus draw us to Himself. We are inherently motivated to have our needs met, but it is extremely easy for us to be deceived into the world's thinking that they can be met in some place other than the hand of God. This can only lead to frustration, because no person, possession, or position can take the place of what God alone can do.

In addition to physical needs like food, clothing, shelter, rest, and protection from danger, we have a set of psychological needs that are related to our sense of personal worth. These have been listed in various ways, but for our purposes it will be helpful to divide them into three major categories.

Love and Acceptance
Everyone needs the security that comes from feeling unconditionally loved and accepted by at least one other individual. A person is incomplete without a sense of belonging and a belief that someone genuinely cares that he or she exists. The problem is that in our life experiences, this need is at best only imperfectly met, and in many cases, almost completely unmet. Direct and indirect *appearance rejection* by parents, peers, and society leads to a sense of *insecurity* and a feeling that we must earn acceptance and love. Some go to great lengths to pursue people's approval (often based on physical appearance), while others try to overlook this area by compensating in one of the others.

Significance and Identity

People need a sense of personal significance and identification with someone or something greater than themselves. They need to feel that they are worthwhile and that life is meaningful. But experiences of *personhood rejection,* whether direct or indirect, threaten one's sense of personal worth and purpose for living. This can lead to feelings of *inferiority* and various attempts to earn significance, often based on status. By finding the right partner, living in the right neighborhood, driving the right car, wearing the right clothes, or having the right friends, many people try to find identity and worth. Those who do not do well in this area may try to excel in one of the others in order to minimize failure.

Competence and Fulfillment

Another universal human need is the sense of competence and fulfillment which comes from the belief that one's life has made a difference and that he or she has accomplished something that will last. This is thwarted by direct and indirect experiences of *performance rejection* that can lead to feelings of personal *inadequacy.* Many people seek to validate their worth and find fulfillment through achievement and performance. This may take the form of academic, musical, and athletic accomplishments, but it is especially prominent as the motivating factor in the pursuit of career success. Once again, those who do not do well in this area may seek to compensate by stressing one of the others.

Thus, people generally seek to validate their personal worth through appearance, status, and talent. Carried far enough, efforts to find love and acceptance lead to sensuality and immorality; efforts to find significance and identity lead to materialism and greed; and efforts to find competence and fulfillment lead to excessive competition and aggression. (In extreme cases, these can lead in turn to perversion, theft, and violence.)

It is deceptive to turn to people, things, and circumstances to meet our needs, because none of these can fully satisfy them. Yet many believers frequently fall into this trap, sometimes applying a Christian veneer over the same futile process used by non-

Christians. God has set eternity in our heart (Ecclesiastes 3:11), and He alone can fill the void. This is not to say that it is wrong to be concerned about our appearance, our possessions, or our accomplishments. Whatever we do as "ambassadors for Christ" (2 Corinthians 5:20) should be characterized by excellence, because it is done to the glory of God (1 Corinthians 10:31; Colossians 3:23). But if our joy and peace depend upon how we look, what we own, or how well we perform, we are not looking to the Creator but rather to the creation to meet our God-given needs.

Exchanged Life Spirituality

GOD'S PLAN TO MEET OUR NEEDS

By trusting in Christ, we are placed in a position where we will be restored to God's ultimate intention for His people. Christ redeemed us by paying the penalty for our sins and delivering us from the bondage of sin.

> In Him we have redemption through His blood, the forgiveness of our trespasses, according to the riches of His grace. (Ephesians 1:7)
>
> For He delivered us from the domain of darkness, and transferred us to the kingdom of His beloved Son, in whom we have redemption, the forgiveness of sins. (Colossians 1:13–14)
>
> And when you were dead in your transgressions and the uncircumcision of your flesh, He made you alive together with Him, having forgiven us all our transgressions, having canceled out the certificate of debt consisting of decrees against us and which was hostile to us; and He has taken it out of the way, having nailed it to the cross. (Colossians 2:13–14)

As a result of our redemption, God's holy demands have been *propitiated* (satisfied) and we have been *justified* (declared righteous) by the living God (Romans 3:24; Titus 3:7); Christ's righteousness has been *imputed* or placed on our account (Romans

5:18–19; 2 Corinthians 5:21). Because the barrier of sin has been removed, we are now *reconciled* to God with full access as His adopted children to call Him "Abba! Father!" (Romans 8:15). Moreover, our old selves have been crucified with Christ, so that we have become identified with Him in His death, burial, resurrection, and ascension to the right hand of the Father (Romans 6:3–11; Galatians 2:20; Ephesians 2:5–6; Colossians 3:1–4). Our former identity in Adam was put to death; our new and eternal identity in Christ became a living reality when we placed our faith in Him.

Without Christ, we were out of harmony with God; life was all about self, and we were driven to use people, things, and circumstances to meet our needs. In Christ, we are in harmony with God; for us as believers, life should be all about the One who has already fully met our needs.

A SPIRITUAL FAMILY

God the Father desires to create a community of spiritual beings to whom He can reveal Himself, from whom He can receive the glory, praise, and honor due His name, and with whom He can give and receive love (Ephesians 1:4–6). This desire is being realized in His plan to create a spiritual family that He can love and accept in eternal fellowship (Galatians 4:4–7; Ephesians 2:19). We are that family, and Christ is the firstborn (Colossians 1:18).

As members of God's family, our need for unconditional love and acceptance is fully met. We are secure in God's limitless love. Even when we were in rebellion against Him as His enemies, He demonstrated His love toward us "in that while we were yet sinners, Christ died for us" (Romans 5:8).

> For I am convinced that neither death, nor life, nor angels, nor principalities, nor things present, nor things to come, nor powers, nor height, nor depth, nor any other created thing, shall be able to separate us from the love of God, which is in Christ Jesus our Lord. (Romans 8:38–39)

> See how great a love the Father has bestowed upon us,
> that we should be called children of God; and such we are.
> (1 John 3:1)

A SPIRITUAL BODY

God the Son desires to create a community of spiritual beings of whom He can be the head, and with whom and through whom He can rule all creation (Ephesians 1:9–10, 22–23). This desire is being realized in His plan to create a spiritual body that has significance and identity as an extension of the incarnation of Christ (Ephesians 1:9–12). We are that body, and Christ is the head (Ephesians 1:22–23; Colossians 1:18).

As individual parts of Christ's body, our need for true significance and identity is fully met. We have meaning and purpose because of who we are in Christ. God did not save us according to our works, "but according to His own purpose and grace which was granted us in Christ Jesus from all eternity" (2 Timothy 1:9).

> But just as it is written, "Things which eye has not seen and ear has not heard, and which have not entered the heart of man, all that God has prepared for those who love Him." (1 Corinthians 2:9)
>
> Blessed be the God and Father of our Lord Jesus Christ, who according to His great mercy has caused us to be born again to a living hope through the resurrection of Jesus Christ from the dead, to obtain an inheritance which is imperishable and undefiled and will not fade away, reserved in heaven for you. (1 Peter 1:3–4)

A SPIRITUAL TEMPLE

God the Holy Spirit desires to create a community of spiritual beings who will receive and reflect the likeness of God and glorify Him forever (Ephesians 2:21–22). This desire is being realized in His plan to create a spiritual temple of living stones into whom He can invest His likeness and power, competent to serve and glorify Him in eternal fulfillment (1 Peter 2:4–5). We are that temple, and

Christ is the cornerstone (Ephesians 2:20).

As living stones in God's temple, our need for lasting competence and fulfillment is fully met. The Holy Spirit has blessed every believer with spiritual gifts, and we have been given the time, opportunities, and abilities to accomplish His purposes for us. The things we do in His power will last forever.

> And for this purpose also I labor, striving according to His power, which mightily works within me. (Colossians 1:29)
>
> That He would grant you, according to the riches of His glory, to be strengthened with power through His Spirit in the inner man. (Ephesians 3:16)

(As an *exercise*, read the following verses to see how they relate to our three personal-worth needs: 1 Corinthians 1:5–9; 2 Corinthians 1:21–22; 2:14; 3:4–6; Galatians 4:4–7; Ephesians 1:6, 9–12, 18; 2:10; 3:11–12, 16–20; 5:2; 6:10–18; Philippians 2:13; Colossians 1:11, 21–22, 27; 3:3; 2 Timothy 1:7; 1 Peter 1:5.)

As Christians, we must look beyond people, things, and circumstances to meet our needs. All of these are unstable and inadequate, and if we depend on them, we will certainly fail. Moving in the direction of the flesh will not meet our needs; at *best* it can only provide a deceptive façade of security and significance. Instead, we must dare to believe that if everything else is taken away, our God is enough. This does not minimize the fact that there will be pain when relationships break down and when failure and rejection occur. These things are painful, but they *will not destroy us* when we derive our self-image from God rather than people. From an ultimate standpoint, we are loved, we are significant, and we are competent, but only in Him, and only in the plan to which He calls us.

Why then do so many believers continue to act as nonbelievers when it comes to the quest for security, meaning, and fulfillment in life? The answer lies in the fact that there are three powerful forces which are opposed to our walking in the Spirit: the flesh, the world, and the devil (Ephesians 2:2–3).

The *flesh* is the power or "law of sin" which is in our members (Romans 7:14–25). It is not the same as the "old self" which was put to death at the cross (Romans 6:6). Although we received a new spirit when we came to Christ, we are still encased in the same body with its physical needs and cravings. Nor was our soul or personality (mind, emotions, and will) instantly transformed. Old attitudes, values, habits, and actions were not eradicated, but continue to surface. Our mental, emotional, and volitional processes must gradually be brought into conformity with the new person we have become in Christ, but this takes time, willingness, and the work of the Holy Spirit. We have been programmed into thinking that our identity is based on what others think or what we think about ourselves rather than what God thinks about us.

This programming is largely a product of the second of the three forces, the *world*. We are constantly being bombarded by a cultural system that promotes values and perspectives that are totally opposed to those of the Bible. Our circumstances are so overwhelmingly real that we lose sight of who we are in Christ. Even though Scripture tells us that we are pilgrims and strangers on earth and that our citizenship is in heaven, we are prone to live our lives as though this physical existence is the supreme reality. Unless we habitually reprogram our minds with the truths of Scripture, we will be profoundly influenced by a culture that tells us to find meaning in hedonism and materialism.

The third force that works against our spiritual life is the *devil*. Satan and his minions utilize the world and the flesh to accomplish their purpose of defeating the lives of Christians and rendering them ineffective. But Satan can only oppress us while we are controlled by the flesh. He cannot defeat the life of Christ in us.

All three of these forces wage war against the spiritual vitality of the believer, and it is essential in this warfare that we cultivate an eternal rather than a temporal perspective. Everything hinges on how we respond to God's plan to satisfy our needs for personal worth.

OUR RESPONSE TO GOD'S PLAN

In Romans 6, Paul describes a threefold process that moves from the inner to the outer man and aligns the believer with spiritual truth. It begins with *knowing* one's identity in Christ (6:3–10), progresses to *reckoning* or considering these truths to be so (6:11), and climaxes with *yielding* or presenting oneself to God (6:12–14).

Knowing

Christians often suffer from spiritual ignorance and amnesia; many believers either do not know or have forgotten who they are in Christ. As a result, their self-image is derived from the wrong source. Using a variation of Luke 9:18–20, there are three fundamental questions we can ask of ourselves:

> Who do you say that you are?
> Who do people say that you are?
> Who does God say that you are?

All too often, our sense of identity is based on our answers to the first two questions rather than the third. When this happens, we will unavoidably arrive at unbiblical conclusions and base our sense of personal worth on the wrong things. As believers in Christ, our identity must not be based on what people say, but on what God says of us. He says that He unconditionally loves and accepts us regardless of how we feel or perform (Romans 5:8). He tells us that we have become "united with Christ in the likeness of His death" and that we will also be united with Him "in the likeness of His resurrection" (Romans 6:5).

Christians know that Christ died for them, but many do not know that they also died in and with Him. We must realize that "our old self was crucified with Him, that our body of sin might be done away with, that we should no longer be slaves to sin; for he who has died is freed from sin" (Romans 6:6–7). It is through our co-crucifixion with Christ that we have died to the bondage of sin, and this is something God has already accomplished. We may not *feel* this is true, but we must never reason from our performance to our position; our security and significance in Christ are not threatened by earthly failure or rejection. Instead, we must base our behavior on our belief. Who we are should determine what we do and not vice versa. Ideally, our behavior will reflect who we are, but it does not make us who we are. Our identity is based on our new birth in Christ. We *have* His righteousness (Philippians 3:9; 2 Corinthians 5:21), and His life is our life.

A firm understanding of our salvation in Romans 1–5 is essential to our growth in sanctification in Romans 6–8.

Reckoning

After Paul describes the reality of our identification with Christ in His death, burial, and resurrection life (Romans 6:3–10), he moves from knowing the truth to believing the truth. "Even so consider yourselves to be dead to sin, but alive to God in Christ Jesus" (Romans 6:11). We must not only learn the truth, but also count it to be so. When the truth is "united by faith" in those who hear (Hebrews 4:2), believers can enjoy God's rest (Hebrews 4:3–10). But this does not happen automatically. We are told to "be diligent to enter that rest" (Hebrews 4:11) by taking hold of truths that we have not fully experienced and believing them in spite of appearances to the contrary. "Sin need have no more power over the believer than he grants it through unbelief. If he is alive unto sin it will be due largely to the fact that he has failed to reckon himself dead unto sin" (Ruth Paxon).

Reckoning is a process that is neither natural nor easy. Most writers who advocate the exchanged life agree that believers often have to come to the end of themselves and of their own resources before they are able to have a genuine realization of their co-crucifixion with Christ. In most cases, it is only when people reach the point of "brokenness" and "surrender" that they are ready to turn from the "self-life" to the "Christ-life." James McConkey observed that "faith is dependence upon God. And this God-dependence only begins when self-dependence ends. And self-dependence only comes to its end, with some of us, when sorrow, suffering, affliction, broken plans and hopes bring us to that place of self-helplessness and defeat." In the university of life, these are not courses anyone would elect to take, since they involve pain and the frightening prospect of the loss of control. (From a biblical point of view, of course, we are only abandoning the *illusion* of control, since we were never really in control of our lives in the first place—we just thought we were.) But as F. B. Meyer put it, "If you are not willing, confess that you are willing to be made willing" (cf. John 7:17). It is only when we surrender full control of our life and plans to Christ that we discover His peace. When we lose our lives for His sake, we find His life instead.

As we "fight the good fight of faith" (1 Timothy 6:12) by reckoning what God has said about our position in Christ to be true, the Holy Spirit will add assurance and make these truths more real in our experience. Thus Paul prayed in Ephesians that God would give his readers "a spirit of wisdom and of revelation in the knowledge of Him" (Ephesians 1:17).

> I pray that the eyes of your heart may be enlightened, so that you may know what is the hope of His calling, what are the riches of the glory of His inheritance in the saints, and what is the surpassing greatness of His power toward us who believe. (Ephesians 1:18–19a)

We should not approach the spiritual life in an academic and theoretical way. God's truth is not merely designed to inform us but also to transform us. We *really have* become new creatures; we are part of a new species with a new heredity and inheritance as children of God and citizens of heaven. We have been removed from death in Adam to life in Christ. Eternal life *is* Christ's life, and we received His life at the time of our spiritual birth (Romans 6:4–6; 8:9; 2 Corinthians 5:14–17; Galatians 2:20; Ephesians 1:4; 2:6, 10; Colossians 1:12–14; 3:1–3; 1 John 3:1–2). Christ is not merely alongside us or in front of us; He is *in* us, and He wants to express His life *through* us. Moreover, the New Testament is even more emphatic that we are *in* Him. We are in a position of victory in Christ who is at the right hand of God (Ephesians 1:20). The epistles do not tell us to *feel* this truth, but to trust and honor God by accepting that it is so. In this way, we start with the character and promises of God and not with ourselves. This is not a matter of passivity (the "let go—let God" idea can be overdone), but of active choice that is energized by divine grace. Nor is this a matter of sinless perfection, but of gradual growth in a context of spiritual warfare against the flesh, the world, and the devil. The flesh (the capacity to live life in our own power rather than in the power of the Spirit) is neither removed nor improved; we will not be rid of this propensity until we are resurrected.

Yielding

As we come to *know* the truth about our identification with Christ and couple it with faith by *reckoning* it to be true, it is important that we act upon it by presenting or *yielding* ourselves to God as new creatures in Christ:

> Therefore do not let sin reign in your mortal body that you should obey its lusts, and do not go on presenting the members of your body to sin as instruments of unrighteousness; but present yourselves to God as those alive from the dead, and your members as instruments of righteousness to God. (Romans 6:12–13)

When we are progressively transformed by the renewing of our minds (Romans 12:2) in the truths of Scripture, our thinking is brought into greater conformity with what God, not the world, says about us. We can present ourselves to God as "those alive from the dead" because we have come to know and believe that this is who we are. In the same way, our bodies can become living and holy sacrifices which are acceptable to God (Romans 12:1) as we present our members to Him as "instruments of righteousness" (Romans 6:13).

If we want our spiritual lives to flourish, this threefold process of knowing, reckoning, and yielding should become a daily habit

(Luke 9:23). It is easier to "unlearn" spiritual truth than it is to learn it. If we do not regularly reinforce this process, it will gradually slip away from us.

As we take God at His word by believing Him in spite of circumstances and appearances to the contrary, we gain a divine perspective on our problems and walk more in His power and less in our own resources. The daily reckoning that we are "dead to sin but alive to God in Christ Jesus" brings us into a deeper understanding that Christ's life is now our life and His destiny is now our destiny. We have exchanged the old for the new, and in Him we have love, meaning, and fulfillment.

Thus we have seen that our true identity is not in our "outer man," but in our "inner man" (2 Corinthians 4:16). We are spiritual beings who are temporarily clothed with the perishable and mortal, but the time is coming when "this perishable must put on the imperishable, and this mortal must put on immortality" (1 Corinthians 15:53). When the Lord returns, what we are outwardly will be perfectly conformed to who we have already become inwardly. Until then, we must set our minds "on the things above, not on the things that are on earth" (Colossians 3:2) and put to death the deeds of the body by walking in conscious dependence on the power of the Spirit (Romans 8:13). We are inherently motivated to have our needs met, but we must continually remind ourselves that they have already been fully met in Christ. This is a truth that can liberate us from the bondage of selfishness and pride. It can free us from being grabbers and allow us to become givers who expect and need nothing in return. As C. S. Lewis observed at the end of *Mere Christianity,*

> Your real, new self (which is Christ's and also yours, and yours just because it is His) will not come as long as you are looking for it. It will come when you are looking for Him.... Give up yourself, and you will find your real self. Lose your life and you will save it.... Keep back nothing. Nothing that you have not given away will ever be really yours. Nothing in you that has not died will ever be raised

from the dead. Look for yourself, and you will find in the long run only hatred, loneliness, despair, rage, ruin, and decay. But look for Christ and you will find Him, and with Him everything else thrown in.

If we try to gratify our needs, we will experience frustration and failure. If we pursue God and hunger and thirst for Him and His righteousness, we will be satisfied (Matthew 5:6) and our needs will be fulfilled. It all reduces to trust: can we trust God as a person and believe that truth is what God says it is, regardless of how we feel? This leads us back to where we began—the character of God. As we affirm the goodness and love of God, we will realize that He is not carrying out His program at our expense, but for our highest good. Disobedience to Him is actually self-destructive, while obedience to His desires is self-fulfilling. Armed with this attitude, we can say *no* to the pull of the flesh, the world, and Satan, and *yes* to Christ in what He calls us to do. When we *respond* to the truth in obedient action, a reciprocal process is set in motion: just as attitude leads to action, so action creates or reinforces attitude. This is not an either/or situation but a both/and syngery. Faith grows as we put it into action. When we begin to *act* as though Christ is living His life through us, we are acting in accordance with biblical reality. This, in turn, makes these truths more real to us, which then makes them easier to act upon, and so forth. At any given time, we are reinforcing either a positive or a negative cycle of attitudes and actions. This is why it is so important to renew our minds with the truths of Scripture on a regular basis and respond to them by choosing to put them into action.

THE LIFE OF CHRIST IN US

The spiritual life is really the *life of Jesus Christ* that has been reproduced in the believer. Christ's life is "resident in, reigning over, and released through the human life" (Jack R. Taylor). "I have been crucified with Christ; and it is no longer I who live, but Christ lives in me; and the life which I now live in the flesh I live by faith in the Son of God, who loved me, and delivered Himself up for me" (Galatians 2:20). Our hearts have become Christ's dwelling place, and this truth grows more real in our awareness and experience as we lay hold of it by faith (Ephesians 3:17). Paul reached the point where he so identified his life with Christ's life that he was able to say from a prison cell in Rome, "For to me, to live is Christ, and to die is gain" (Philippians 1:21). This is the goal of the Christian life—a growing understanding of our union with Christ both in our thinking and in our practice.

Jesus summed it up in these simple but profound words in John 14:20: "You in Me, and I in you." The "you in me" refers to our relationship with Christ by virtue of our life in Him. The "I in you" speaks of our fellowship with Christ by virtue of His life in us. The former relates to our position or standing; the latter relates to our practice or state. Our relationship with God is actual—it was determined by our spiritual *birth* in Christ. Our fellowship with God is potential—it is developed by our spiritual *growth* in Christ.

These spiritual truths have been well summarized in this way:

Jesus Christ gave His life for you…[Salvation]
so that He could give His life to you…[Sanctification]
so that He could live His life through you. [Service]

We cannot produce biological or spiritual life; we were created to *receive* spiritual life and to display it. Nevertheless, Scripture exhorts us to "grow in the grace and knowledge of our Lord and Savior Jesus Christ" (2 Peter 3:18). This involves an ongoing process of walking in fellowship with God in obedient response to the light of His Word. Growth in our apprehension and application of our identity in Christ is not uniform. As in nature, so also in the spiritual life—there are spurts of growth followed by periods of relative dormancy. There are no experiential shortcuts on the path to maturity in Christlikeness.

If we say that we have fellowship with Him and yet walk in the darkness, we lie and do not practice the truth; but

if we walk in the light as He Himself is in the light, we
have fellowship with one another, and the blood of Jesus
His son cleanses us from all sin. (1 John 1:6–7)

When we succumb to temptation in thought, word, or deed,
we are living beneath the dignity of the new identity we have
received in Christ Jesus. When the light of Scripture reveals areas
of sin, we must respond to the light by confessing our sins so that
we can continue to enjoy fellowship with the God of light and holiness. "If we confess our sins, He is faithful and righteous to forgive
us our sins and to cleanse us from all unrighteousness" (1 John
1:9). From a biblical point of view, it is not normal for Christians
to live in defeat, especially when cleansing and fellowship are so
readily available. As we abide in Christ, His life in us can qualita-
tively affect every aspect of our earthly existence, including our
family, work, thoughts, attitudes, and speech.

LEGALISM, LICENSE, AND LIBERTY

The spiritual life is a balance between the twin extremes of legalism and license. *Legalism* is striving in the effort of the flesh to
achieve a human standard of righteousness. It is easy to be vic-
timized by the pharisaic attitude that equates spirituality with conformity to an artificial code of behavior. Confusing the standards
of Christians with Christian standards, many believers think that
following a set of do's and don'ts leads to personal holiness.

Legalism emphasizes an external set of rules and prohibitions
rather than the inner life in the Spirit. Because of the influence of
a number of Judaizers, the Galatians fell into this error when they
exchanged their freedom in Christ for the yoke of the law
(Galatians 5:1–8). In his corrective epistle to the Galatians, Paul
stressed the crucial truth that the same principle that *saves* a believer (grace through faith) also *sanctifies* a believer.

This is the only thing I want to find out from you: did
you receive the Spirit by the works of the Law, or by hear-
ing with faith? Are you so foolish? Having begun by the

Spirit, are you now being perfected by the flesh? (Galatians 3:2–3)

For sin shall not be master over you, for you are not under law but under grace. (Romans 6:14)

But now we have been released from the Law, having died to that by which we were bound, so that we serve in newness of the Spirit and not in oldness of the letter. (Romans 7:6)

	LAW	GRACE
Says...	Do	Done
Emphasizes...	What we do	What God does
Lives out of...	The flesh (self-life)	The Spirit (Christ-life)
Draws on...	Our resources	God's resources
Deals with...	External rules, regulations, standards	Inner heart attitude
Primary focus...	Ought to, should, must	Want to
Creates...	Bondage, duty, obligation	Freedom
Lives life from the...	Outside-in	Inside-out
Declares...	Do in order to be	You are; therefore do
Produces...	Guilt and condemnation	Acceptance and security
Leads to...	Defeat	Victory

Christian growth is not achieved by outer rules or ritual, but by an inner relationship. Christlikeness is developed "through the Spirit, by faith" (Galatians 5:5).

While legalism promotes a "do what you have to do" mentality, *license*, the opposite extreme, is characterized by "do what you want to do." This stems from an attitude that takes the grace of God for granted and minimizes the consequences of sin (Romans 6:1, 15). "I know I'm not living the Christian life now, but maybe I'll get back into that later—at least I'll get into heaven." Christians can easily get locked into the quest for pleasure, prosperity, popularity, or power. But the cost of success in these areas often entails a compromise in personal integrity and morality.

The biblical balance between the excesses of legalism and license is *liberty*. Instead of doing what we have to do or doing as we please, we have the true freedom in Christ to do as He pleases. Liberty in Christ stresses inner transformation as the key to outer manifestation. Growth in grace is accomplished by knowing and depending upon the person of God. Lack of divine blessing comes from unbelief, not from failure of devotion. "To preach devotion first, and blessing second, is to reverse God's order, and preach law, not grace. The Law made man's blessing depend on devotion; Grace confers undeserved, unconditional blessing: our devotion may follow, but does not always do so—in proper measure" (William Newell).

Only as bondslaves of Christ do we have real liberty. But freedom always entails responsibilities and consequences (Galatians 6:7–8). We must not only know the truth, but put it into practice.

OUR POSITION	OUR PRACTICE
Romans 1–11	Romans 12–16
Ephesians 1–3	Ephesians 4–6
Colossians 1–2	Colossians 3–4
Belief	Behavior
Who we are	What we do
Attitudes	Actions
Standing	State
Being	Becoming
Determined	Developing
Spiritual wealth	Spiritual walk
Birth in Christ	Growth in Christ
Based on Christ's death	Based on Christ's life
Our relationship with God	Our fellowship with God
By grace through faith	By grace through faith

By position, we mean *who we actually are* in Christ Jesus at this very moment; we do not need to wait until we see Him for it to be true of us. Having entered by faith into the new life that is available in Christ, we are called as members of God's family to grow in such a way that our practice conforms more and more to our position in the heavenly places in Christ. This is the process of the spiritual life, and the basis of this process is our new identity in Christ.

This movement from position to practice is the most difficult aspect of the spiritual life. Other chapters in this book address the central question of how we can get our faith to work in the nitty-gritty details of everyday living.

Motivated Spirituality

WHY DO WE DO WHAT WE DO?
NO OTHER OPTION? FEAR?

What motivates people to behave the way they do? Why do we sometimes avoid evil and at other times choose it? Or from another perspective, why do we do the right thing on some occasions and fail to do it on others?

People are motivated to satisfy their needs for security, significance, and fulfillment, but they turn to the wrong places to get their needs met. This chapter will present the option of looking to Christ rather than the world to meet our needs. Our task is to be more motivated by the things God declares to be important than by the things the world says are important.

Because believers have a new nature and are indwelled by the Spirit of God, they have more options than unbelievers. They can choose to walk by the Spirit and do things that are pleasing to God, whereas those who do not know Christ cannot please God, since even their good deeds are tainted by the fallen nature. "The heart is more deceitful than all else and is desperately sick; who can understand it?" (Jeremiah 17:9). "For all of us have become like one who is unclean, and all our righteous deeds are like a filthy garment" (Isaiah 64:6). "They turn, but not upward, they are like a deceitful bow" (Hosea 7:16). "For from within, out of the heart of men, proceed the evil thoughts, fornications, thefts, murders, adulteries, deeds of coveting and wickedness, as well as deceit, sensuality, envy, slander, pride and foolishness. All these evil things proceed from within and defile the man" (Mark 7:21–23).

VERTICAL AND HORIZONTAL MOTIVATORS

The Bible tells us that the problem with the human condition is internal and that the only solution is a changed heart. The transformation available through new birth in Christ is wrought from the inside out, so that in Christ we become new creatures. Nevertheless, while we are in this body and in this world, believers are still susceptible to the same influences that exert a pull on unbelievers. Worldly or temporal motivators include fear of loss, guilt, pride, hope of personal gain, reputation, prestige, and pleasure. These are "horizontal" motivators, since they are related to the short-term dynamics of the visible and the now. Biblical motivators, however, are more "vertical" since they relate to the long-term dynamics of the invisible and the not-yet. It is not surprising, then, that believers find it easier to be prompted by the former than by the latter. Even when our actions are based upon thinking rather than emotions, it is natural for our thinking to be shaped by a temporal and human perspective. It is only as we yield ourselves to the lordship of Christ and renew our minds with spiritual truth that our thought life will be shaped by an eternal and godly perspective.

At first, the biblical motivators seem remote and external, but as we press on in the process of spiritual maturity and growth in Christ, they become more real and internal. But this is a gradual process, and it is never completed in this brief earthly sojourn. While we are in this world we will never arrive at a perfect motivational structure; instead, we will find ourselves pulled by the natural and the spiritual. This is why it is important to avoid the paralysis of analysis—if we waited until we had entirely perfect and unalloyed motives before we acted, we would probably do nothing at all!

At this point, I have distinguished seven motivators in Scripture, but it would be easy to argue that some should be combined or that others should be added. Nonetheless, here are the motivators that we will discuss in view of their implications for our lives:

1. *No other options.* When we come to Christ, we are effectively admitting the inadequacy of every other approach to life. While this is a negative motivator, it can have real power in times of doubt and pain.

2. *Fear.* This can be both negative (fear of consequences) and positive (fear of God).

3. *Love and gratitude.* This is a frequently cited motive that is positive in nature.

4. *Rewards.* Scripture talks much more about rewards as incentives for faithfulness and obedience than we might suppose.

5. *Our identity in Christ.* This should have profound implications for our behavior.

6. *Purpose and hope.* It is important for us to cultivate a biblical purpose for living and a hope that is founded on the character of God.

7. *Longing for God.* The vision of God has been a recurring theme in devotional literature, though it is not as common in the Christian literature of our own century.

These seven biblical realities can keep us in the process of walking with Christ in the context of life's ambiguities and uncertainties. Some of these may be relevant at certain times and uncompelling at others. In some situations, we may be prompted by more than one of them, and in other situations we may act without being consciously aware of any of them. Our actions, even when related to areas of ministry, are often based on an alloy of temporal and biblical motivations.

By looking at the list, you can see that these motivators relate to different stages and aspects of the spiritual journey, and that some may seem to be more accessible than others. For instance, we may be able to identify more with number 3 than with number 7. But remember that they are all facets of the same gem, since they are integrated in the character and promises of the living God. In a sense, they are components of a single passion—a concern for one thing above all else, the one thing most needed (Luke 10:41–42). When we are not propelled and impelled by one ultimate attraction, we are pulled by multiple desires. The worries of the world, the deceitfulness of riches, and the desires for other things (Mark 4:19) can choke the word in our lives and prevent us from bearing lasting fruit. When we turn from the lures of the world to the Person of Christ, we discover "the magnet that draws, the anchor that steadies, the fortress that defends, the light that illumines, the treasure that enriches, the law that commands, and the power that enables" (Alexander Maclaren).

NO OTHER OPTIONS

The first of these biblical motivators is entirely negative in nature, but there are times when it can become the only thing that keeps us anchored to the process of obedience. This reality is best illustrated in the aftermath of Jesus' controversial discourse on the bread of life in the sixth chapter of the Gospel of John. When the Lord said, "I am the living bread that came down out of heaven; if anyone eats of this bread, he shall live forever; and the bread also which I shall give for the life of the world is My flesh" (John 6:51), His audience was repulsed by the thought of cannibalism. Their sense of revulsion increased when Jesus added these words: "He who eats My flesh and drinks My blood has eternal life, and I will raise him up on the last day. For My flesh is true food, and My blood is true drink. He who eats My flesh and drinks My blood abides in Me, and I in him" (John 6:54–56).

These mysterious words caused many of His disciples to stumble, and they began to argue with one another. John goes on to say that "as a result of this many of His disciples withdrew, and were not walking with Him anymore. Jesus said therefore to the twelve, 'You do not want to go away also, do you?' Simon Peter answered Him, 'Lord, to whom shall we go? You have words of eternal life. And we have believed and have come to know that You are the Holy One of God'" (John 6:66–69).

I seriously doubt that Peter had a clearer understanding of Jesus' difficult statements than the many disciples who withdrew from Him. The difference is that while the disciples who left were simply curious or even convinced, Peter and the other disciples who continued to walk with Jesus were committed. Their commitment to the Lord extended beyond their mental grasp, because they had learned to trust Him even when they could not understand Him. But Peter and the others who stayed with Jesus understood this much: at the point when they committed their lives to Him, there was no turning back. They realized that nothing else in this world would do, and that there was no where else they could go.

In the same way, when we give our lives to Christ, we are in effect acknowledging the same thing. To come to Him means to abandon every alternative and to admit the bankruptcy of all other approaches to meaning, value, and purpose in life.

In a universe without God, there is no source of ultimate *meaning.* As I discuss in *I'm Glad You Asked,* the universe is expanding, and left to itself, the galaxies will grow farther apart and the stars will eventually burn out. All will be cold, dark, and lifeless. On the scale of cosmic time, the human race (let alone the life of an individual) flashes into existence for the briefest moment before passing into nothingness. From an ultimate standpoint, all that we do is meaningless, since no one will be left to remember in the endless cosmic night. Without God and immortality, our life, and indeed, that of the whole human race, is merely an episode between two oblivions. We may have the illusion of meaning because others are still around, but in the long run, all of us will disappear, and our work and sacrifice will make no difference to an impersonal and indifferent cosmos.

Similarly, without a personal God, there is no basis for *morality,* since values such as right and wrong are totally relative and have no absolute mooring. If we are the product of an accidental combination of molecules in an ultimately impersonal universe, human values such as honesty, brotherhood, love, and equality have no more cosmic significance than treachery, selfishness, hatred, and prejudice.

We are also stripped of *purpose* in a godless reality. An impersonal universe is bereft of purpose and plan; in the final analysis it moves only toward decay, disorder, and death. It is Macbeth's "tale told by an idiot, full of sound and fury, signifying nothing." We may try to embrace short-term purposes, but seen from the larger perspective, they are pointless, because the universe itself is pointless.

Few people have thought through these logical implications of a world without God, and no one can live consistently with them. All of us act as though human existence has meaning, as though moral values are real, and as though human life has purpose and dignity. That is, they act as though God exists, since all these things presuppose an infinite-personal Creator.

In spite of this, even as believers we may be tempted in difficult times to question the validity of following Christ and living in obedience to Scripture. We may wonder if it is really worth it all. It is in times like these when this negative motivator may be the only thread that holds us in contact with reality—where else can we go? Either Christ is the way, the truth, and the life, or He is not; there is nothing in between. And if He is who He claims to be, there is no genuine way, no absolute truth, and no eternal life apart from Him. The honesty of admitting this during times of trial and loss can help us cling to God even when there appears to be no positive reason for doing so. To paraphrase a line in C. S. Lewis's *The Screwtape Letters,* Satan's cause is never more in danger than when a human, no longer desiring, but still intending to do God's will, looks round upon a universe from which every trace of Him seems to have vanished and asks why he has been forsaken and still obeys.

THE FEAR OF THE LORD

> For we must all appear before the judgment seat of Christ, that each one may be recompensed for his deeds in the body, according to what he has done, whether good or bad. Therefore knowing the fear of the Lord, we persuade men. (2 Corinthians 5:10–11a)

We hear little about the fear of the Lord in our time, and it is hardly in evidence in the community of believers as a source of behavioral motivation. But even a superficial concordance study will reveal that the fear of God is highly prized not only in the Old Testament but also in the New. Paul's statement above makes it clear that the fear of the Lord is a solid component in his motivational structure. It is part of the reason that he suffered so much in the process of persuading people about the good news of forgiveness and newness of life in Christ Jesus. (Compare this with his statement in 1 Corinthians 9:16: "Woe is me if I do not preach the gospel.")

What does it mean to fear God? Consider Jesus' words to the multitude that gathered to hear Him: "And I say to you, My friends, do not be afraid of those who kill the body, and after that have no more that they can do. But I will warn you whom to fear: fear the One who after He has killed has authority to cast into hell; yes, I tell you, fear Him!" (Luke 12:4–5). Although the living and omnipotent God is worthy of far more reverence than we accord to men, Jesus knows that our natural tendency is to be more concerned about the opinions and responses of people whom we can see than about the favor of God whom we cannot see. Jesus' words remind us that succumbing to this tendency to play to the visible over the invisible is a serious mistake, because the consequences of disobedience to God are so much greater than the consequences of disobedience to men. God's authority is absolute, and our ultimate disposition is in His hands alone. Therefore, anything short of absolute surrender to His claims on our lives is a misguided attempt at autonomy, and this is a game we can never win.

But what are we to make of the apostle John's familiar words in 1 John 4:18? "There is no fear in love; but perfect love casts out fear, because fear involves punishment, and the one who fears is not perfected in love." John has been describing the confidence we have in the day of judgment as believers in Christ, knowing that we are the recipients of the love of God. This love dispels the terror of condemnation and assures us that we abide in Christ because He has given us of His Spirit (4:13). But John is not dispelling the need for a holy awe and reverence of God. Indeed, when he saw the glorified Christ in Revelation 1, he fell at His feet as a dead man. At that point, the Lord laid His right hand upon him and said, "Do not be afraid: I am the first and the last, and the living One; and I was dead, and behold, I am alive forevermore, and I have the keys of death and of Hades" (Revelation 1:17–18).

The Old and New Testaments clearly relate the fear of God to knowing Him, loving Him, obeying Him, and honoring Him: "And Moses said to the people, 'Do not be afraid; for God has come in order to test you, and in order that the fear of Him may remain with you, so that you may not sin'" (Exodus 20:20). "Oh that they had such a heart in them, they would fear Me, and keep all My commandments always, that it may be well with them and with their sons forever" (Deuteronomy 5:29). "You shall fear only the Lord your God; and you shall worship Him, and swear by His name" (Deuteronomy 6:13). "And now, Israel, what does the Lord your God require from you, but to fear the Lord your God, to walk in all His ways and love Him, and to serve the Lord your God with all your heart and with all your soul" (Deuteronomy 10:12). "Behold, the fear of the Lord, that is wisdom; and to depart from evil is understanding" (Job 28:28). "The secret of the Lord is for those who fear Him, and He will make them know His covenant" (Psalm 25:14). "For great is the Lord, and greatly to be praised; He is to be feared above all gods" (Psalm 96:4). "If You, Lord, should mark iniquities, O Lord, who could stand? But there is forgiveness with You, that You may be feared" (Psalm 130:3–4). "Do not be wise in your own eyes; fear the Lord and turn away from evil" (Proverbs 3:7). "But for you who fear My name the sun of righteousness will rise with healing in its wings" (Malachi 4:2). "Then those who feared the Lord spoke to one another, and the Lord gave attention and heard it, and a book of remembrance was written before Him for those who fear the Lord and who esteem His name" (Malachi 3:16). "So the church…enjoyed peace, being built up; and, going on in the fear of the Lord and in the comfort of the Holy Spirit, it continued to increase" (Acts 9:31). "Therefore, having these promises, beloved, let us cleanse ourselves from all defilement of flesh and spirit, perfecting holiness in the fear of God" (2 Corinthians 7:1). "Be subject to one another in the fear of Christ" (Ephesians 5:21). "Work out your salvation with fear and trembling" (Philippians 2:12). "Therefore, let us fear lest, while a promise remains of entering His rest, any one of you should seem to have come short of it" (Hebrews 4:1). "And if you address as Father the One who impartially judges according to each man's work, conduct yourselves in fear during the time of your stay upon earth" (1 Peter 1:17). "Fear God, and give Him glory, because the hour of His judgment has come; and worship Him who made the heaven and the earth and sea and springs of waters" (Revelation 14:7). "Who will not fear, O Lord, and glorify Your name? For You alone are holy" (Revelation 15:4). "Give praise to our God, all you His bondservants, you who fear Him, the small and the great" (Revelation 19:5).

The fear of the Lord not only means the cultivation of a reverential awe of God, but also relates to the mind-set of a subject in a great kingdom. It is the recognition that the King has all power and authority in His hand, and that the subject's life, occupation, and future are dependent on the good pleasure of the King. It is the ongoing acknowledgment of His sovereignty and the truth that our lives are in His hands. It is the foundation for wisdom because it leads to a sense of profound dependency, submission, and trust.

A deepening understanding that we are Christ's bondservants should be part of our motivational structure (see Luke 17:7–10). It can draw us away from the folly of trusting in people more than trusting in God. "Cursed is the man who trusts in mankind and makes flesh His strength, and whose heart turns away from the Lord.... Blessed is the man who trusts in the Lord" (Jeremiah 17:5, 7). It is a fundamental spiritual blunder to be more concerned about pleasing people than about pleasing God, and to be more afraid of human disapproval than divine disapproval.

We would be wise to cultivate a holy fear, awe, and wonder before the magnificence, might, glory, and greatness of the Creator and Ruler of heaven and earth. Like John, when we see the glorified Christ, what we now dimly perceive about His powers and perfections will become much more clear. Perhaps we will react as did two of the animals in *The Wind in the Willows* when they saw the "Piper at the Gate of Dawn":

> "Rat!" he found breath to whisper, shaking. "Are you afraid?"
>
> "Afraid?" murmured the Rat, his eyes shining with unutterable love. "Afraid! Of *Him?* O, never, never! And yet—and yet—O Mole, I am afraid!"
>
> Then the two animals, crouching to the earth, bowed their heads and did worship.

"The fear of the Lord is the beginning of wisdom, and the knowledge of the Holy One is understanding" (Proverbs 9:10).

Motivated Spirituality

WHY DO WE DO WHAT WE DO?
LOVE AND GRATITUDE?
REWARDS?

LOVE AND GRATITUDE

The third biblical motivator is more positive in nature: it is the
response of love and gratitude for who God is and all the wonderful things He has done for us. The Bible is clear that God's love
for us is always previous to our love for Him. "The one who does
not love does not know God, for God is love. By this the love of
God was manifested in us, that God has sent His only begotten
Son into the world so that we might live through Him. In this is
love, not that we loved God, but that He loved us and sent His
Son to be the propitiation for our sins" (1 John 4:8–10). The infinite and unchanging Source of love reached down to us even
when we were His enemies in our foolish rebellion against His
Person and purposes. "But God demonstrates His own love
toward us, in that while we were yet sinners, Christ died for us"
(Romans 5:8). Someone once put it this way: "I asked Jesus how
much he loved me. He stretched out His arms and said, 'This
much'—and died." Jesus loved us when we were unlovable and
unworthy of His attention and care. Because of His agonizing
work as our sinbearer, the way has been opened for those who
were "formerly alienated and hostile in mind, engaged in evil
deeds" (Colossians 1:21) to become God's beloved children,
members of His royal family forever. This love humbles us because
it is undeserved, but it elevates us because it means that when we
come to God by entrusting ourselves to His Son, nothing we do

can separate us from His love (Romans 8:38–39).

The more we come to grasp and enter into this divine love, the more we will want to reciprocate by loving and honoring the eternal Lover of our souls. As John writes, "We love, because He first loved us" (1 John 4:19). The security and significance of God's unquenchable love gives us a basis for responding with love for God and expressing that love in tangible ways through acts of loving service to others. In His Upper Room Discourse Jesus said, "Just as the Father has loved Me, I have also loved you; abide in My love. If you keep My commandments, you will abide in My love; just as I have kept My Father's commandments, and abide in His love" (John 15:9–10). There is a mutual relationship between abiding in the love of Christ and keeping His commandments. When we dwell in the sphere of His unmerited love, we begin to see that His commandments are not burdensome but liberating. Abiding in His love, we become more inclined to obey Him not only because it is in our own best interests, but because it is pleasing to Him. Thus the apostle Paul wrote, "We have as our ambition, whether at home or absent, to be pleasing to Him" (2 Corinthians 5:9). The ambitions of this world are directly or indirectly tied to self-aggrandizement, but the ambition of a true disciple is not exaltation of the self but exaltation of Christ. As we grow in discipleship, our motivational structure is shaped more and more by Christ's love for us and our developing love for Him ("For the love of Christ controls us." 2 Corinthians 5:14). This relationship is reciprocal: the more we love Him, the more we will desire to obey Him; the more we obey Him, the more we will grow in our personal knowledge and love for Him.

Let me offer two questions that can help you assess where you are in this spiritual journey: 1) Do you love God more for Himself than for His gifts and benefits? 2) Are you more motivated to seek His glory and honor than you are to seek your own? These questions are pivotal, not trivial, and I would encourage you to make them a matter of prayerful reflection rather than casual notice. If you cannot honestly answer yes to either of them, do not be disheartened, but ask yourself a third question: 3) Do you want your answer to be yes? If so, offer this intention to the Lord as the desire of your heart, for with such offerings He is pleased. But there is a fourth question that follows hard on the heels of the third: 4) Since this level of commitment always costs, are you willing to pay the price? "If you love Me, you will keep My commandments.... He who has My commandments and keeps them, he it is who loves Me; and he who loves Me shall be loved by My Father, and I will love him, and will disclose Myself to him.... If anyone loves Me, he will keep My word; and My Father will love him, and We will come to him, and make Our abode with him. He who does not love Me does not keep My words" (John 14:15, 21, 23–24). The cost of obedience will take many forms, but if we commit ourselves to loving Jesus, He will give us the needed grace.

Gratitude is closely related to love, since both are based on God's gracious character and the expression of His character in the many benefits He has showered upon us. If we consider the depth and breadth of God's care and blessings in our lives, we will realize that it is only right that we should give thanks in everything (1 Thessalonians 5:18). Sadly, however, we are more inclined to view our lives in terms of what we lack than in view of what we have already received. Instead of seeing the fullness of what we have received in Christ, we tend to approach our experiences from a deficiency perspective. Our gratitude ages quickly when we overlook God's gifts, take them for granted, or regard them as our due.

We would be wise to keep a grateful memory alive by periodically reviewing what once was, what might have been, and what could well be again apart from the grace of God. We should be amazed and thankful for the multitude of good things in our lives, including the ones we often overlook such as food and covering, health, freedom, friends, open access to the Scriptures, and most of all, the riches available to us in a relationship with Christ Jesus. As our gratitude for who God is and what He has done begins to grow, it becomes a meaningful source of motivation for service to our Lord and to others.

Gratitude for what God has done for us in the past can also motivate us to trust Him in the present for what He is going to do in the future. John of Avila observed that "One act of thanksgiving when things go wrong is worth a thousand thanks when things go right." When we develop the habit of recounting the blessings we have received as God's beloved children, we become more inclined to view the hardships and disappointments we face from a long-term, "Romans 8:18, 28" stance. Love and gratitude are healthy biblical motivators that can help us stay in the process of growth in Christlikeness.

REWARDS

Scripture teaches universal accountability before God—all people will be required to give an account to their Creator, but there will be a significant difference between God's judgment of believers and unbelievers. Entrance into heaven is solely a matter of the grace of God and not of works, since "all have sinned and fall short of the glory of God" (Romans 3:23). God's justice would mean that all would be eternally separated from the holiness of God, but God's grace offers us far more than justice requires.

Scripture also affirms that the experience of heaven and hell will not be uniform, since there are degrees of punishment (e.g., Luke 12:47–48; Matthew 11:21–24), and, as we will see, degrees of reward. While salvation is by grace, rewards in the kingdom of heaven are based on works. This means that the quality of our life on this planet has eternal consequences, and that how we live in this temporal realm will have a direct bearing on the quality of eternity.

Whether we like it or not, each one of us is accountable to God, and no one will escape His righteous judgment. Unbelievers will face the great white throne judgment (Revelation 20:11–15) and will be judged on the basis of their works. Believers will stand before the judgment seat of Christ (2 Corinthians 5:10) where their works will also be judged (1 Corinthians 3:10–15). The difference is that there is "no condemnation for those who are in Christ Jesus" (Romans 8:1; see John 5:24) since Christ bore their judgment and gave them His life. Nevertheless, the judgment seat of Christ is not a trivial matter since it can involve loss as well as reward in the kingdom of heaven. I sometimes put it this way: "it's easy to lip-synch in the chorus of life, but each of us will have to sing solo before God."

When we come to Christ, He becomes the foundation of our life and the basis of our entrance into heaven. The superstructure we build upon the foundation consists of our works which are "gold, silver, precious stones, wood, hay, straw" (1 Corinthians 3:12). At the judgment seat, the entire superstructure is set on fire to test the quality of each one's work. We will be rewarded for that which endures the test of purgation (gold, silver, precious stones) and suffer loss for that which is burned up (wood, hay, straw). In view of the fact that believers can be disqualified from rewards through lack of faithfulness or receive the approval of God because of faithfulness (see 1 Corinthians 9:25–27; Philippians 3:10–14; 2 Timothy 2:12; 4:7–8; James 3:1), it is perilous to live in complacency as though we will avoid a day of reckoning.

Thus, fear of loss and hope of reward are two legitimate biblical motivators, and our Lord stressed their importance on multiple occasions (e.g., Matthew 6:19–20; 19:27–30; Luke 12:42–44; John 12:25–26; Revelation 22:12). In three of His parables, Jesus illuminated the condition for rewards and revealed that it is quite different from the criteria the world uses to determine compensation. According to the parable of the vineyard in Matthew 20:1–16, rewards are not based on the amount of time one labors in God's vineyard. It is the providence of God that determines the amount of this world's goods and the length of time we are entrusted with. Our responsibility relates to the way we invest the time we have been granted, whether we are given one or seventy years after our conversion to Christ.

The parable of the talents in Matthew 25:14–30 and the parable of the minas in Luke 19:11–27 teach us that rewards are based neither on the gifts and abilities we have received nor on the level of our productivity. Instead, they are determined by the degree of our faithfulness to the opportunities we have been given. If rewards were based on time, talent, or treasure, those who are relatively rich in these assets would be rewarded for possessing things that actually come from the providential hand of God. The fact that rewards are based on faithfulness to the assets and opportunities we have been given is the divine equalizer that gives every believer, regardless of economic, social, intellectual, or vocational status, the possibility of being approved by God.

Faithfulness relates to the issue of stewardship of the assets and resources of another. I see five facets of stewardship that include not only time, talent, and treasure, but also truth and relationships. Here again, the question is not how much truth we have been exposed to or the size of our relational influence, but what we are doing with the truth and the people God has given us. Faithfulness in the New Testament also relates to the degree of our obedience to God's precepts and principles as revealed in Scripture (including our participation in the Great Commission) as well as the way we respond to the circumstances in which we have been placed. God's approval relates more to the focus of our heart than to the measurable achievements that are usually associated with what our world calls success.

Although Scripture frequently encourages us to pursue reward with God, it tells us little about the nature and content of that reward. I believe the principal reason for this is that in our present state, we are limited in our capacity to grasp the real nature of heavenly rewards (1 Corinthians 2:9). But we can be well assured that they will be worth any temporal sacrifice to gain. In my own theological reflection, I currently identify three areas that appear to be related to rewards. The first of these is greater responsibility in the kingdom of heaven (Luke 16:10–12; 19:17–19). Believers will evidently be granted different spheres of authority based on their faithfulness on earth. The second area is the degree to which we reflect and display the glory and character of God. "And those who have insight will shine brightly like the brightness of the expanse of heaven, and those who lead the many to righteousness, like the stars forever and ever" (Daniel 12:2–3; cf. 1 Corinthians 15:40–41; 2 Corinthians 3:13–18). We are not called to glorify ourselves but to receive and display the glory of the majestic perfections of the infinite and wondrous God of all creation. The third area relates to our capacity to know and experience God. I believe there must be some continuity between the relationships we develop with God and others on earth and the corresponding relationships we will experience in heaven. There are always consequences to relational intimacy and distance; those who cultivate a growing appetite for the experiential knowledge of God in this life will surely know Him better in the next life than those who kept God in the periphery of their earthly interests. As A. W. Tozer put it, "Every Christian will become at last what his desires have made him. We are the sum total of our hungers. The great saints have all had thirsting hearts. Their cry has been, 'My soul thirsteth for God, for the living God: when shall I come and appear before God?' Their longing after God all but consumed them; it propelled them onward and upward to heights toward which less ardent Christians look with languid eye and entertain no hope of reaching." I can conceive of nothing more significant and compelling than the beatific vision of the living God, and if our capacity for this vision relates to faithfulness in this life, every other concern should pale in comparison.

Since there will be a day of reckoning, we would be wise to order our lives with this truth in mind. The Bible calls us away from a mind-set of complacency to the pursuit of discipleship and fruit-bearing. It cautions us not to be seduced by the things our culture declares to be important, because "that which is highly esteemed among men is detestable in the sight of God" (Luke 16:15). The vast bulk of what the world tells us to pursue is directly related to the opinions of others. But in the end, people's opinions will be irrelevant; when we stand before God, only His opinion will matter.

It has been observed that the apostle Paul really had only two days on his calendar: today and *that* day (the day he would stand before Christ), and he lived every "today" in light of "that day." He reveled in God's great gift of justification and encouraged believers to grow in sanctification, but his great hope was in God's promise of glorification. "I consider that the sufferings of this present time are not worthy to be compared with the glory that is to be revealed to us" (Romans 8:18). "Therefore we do not lose heart, but though our outer man is decaying, yet our inner man is being renewed day by day. For momentary, light affliction is producing for us an eternal weight of glory far beyond all comparison, while we look not at the things which are see, but at the things which are not seen; for the things which are seen are temporal, but the things which are not seen are eternal" (2 Corinthians 4:16–18). "For our citizenship is in heaven, from which also we eagerly wait for a Savior, the Lord Jesus Christ; who will transform the body of our humble state into conformity with the body of His glory, by the exertion of the power that He has even to subject all things to Himself" (Philippians 3:20–21). "I have fought the good fight, I have finished the course, I have kept the faith; in the future there is laid up for me the crown of righteousness, which the Lord, the righteous Judge, will award to me on that day; and not only to me, but also to all who have loved His appearing" (2 Timothy 4:7–8).

The Scriptures teach that it is not mercenary to be motivated by reward; instead, Jesus encouraged us to long to hear the words, "Well done, good and faithful servant; enter into the joy of your Lord." The New Testament is replete with exhortations to pursue God's rewards, affirming that they are more than worth the cost. "Blessed is a man who perseveres under trial; for once he has been approved, he will receive the crown of life, which the Lord has promised to those who love Him" (James 1:12). "And without faith it is impossible to please Him, for he who comes to God must believe that He is, and that He is a rewarder of those who seek Him.… [Moses considered] the reproach of Christ greater riches than the treasures of Egypt, for he was looking to the reward" (Hebrews 11:6, 26). "Beloved, now we are children of God, and it has not appeared as yet what we shall be. We know that, when He appears, we shall be like Him, because we shall see Him just as He is. And everyone who has this hope fixed on Him purifies himself, just as He is pure" (1 John 3:2–3).

C. S. Lewis argued in his marvelous sermon *The Weight of Glory* that our problem is not that our desires are too strong, but that they are too weak. "We are half-hearted creatures, fooling about with drink and sex and ambition when infinite joy is offered us, like an ignorant child who wants to go on making mud pies in a slum because he cannot imagine what is meant by the offer of a holiday at the sea. We are far too easily pleased." In comparison to what God wants to give us, the best this world can offer is toys, trinkets, and tinsel.

We should be motivated by the fact that right now we are in the process of becoming what we will be in eternity. We should give it everything we have, because eternal gain will be worth anything we sacrificed in our brief earthly sojourn.

REFLECTION

I used to think—
Loving life so greatly—
That to die would be
Like leaving a party
Before the end.

Now I know that the party
Is really happening
Somewhere else;
That the light and the music—
Escaping in snatches
To make the pulse beat
And the tempo quicken—
Come from a long way
Away.

And I know too
That when I get there
The music will never
End.

EVANGELINE PATERSON

CHAPTER 12

Motivated Spirituality

WHY DO WE DO WHAT WE DO?
OUR IDENTITY IN CHRIST?
PURPOSE AND HOPE?

OUR IDENTITY IN CHRIST

Joe Louis was the world heavyweight boxing champion from 1937 until he retired in 1949. During his time of service in the army, Louis was driving with a fellow GI when he was involved in a minor collision with a large truck. The truck driver got out, yelling and swearing at Louis, who just sat in the driver's seat, smiling. "Why didn't you get out and knock him flat?" asked his buddy after the truck driver had moved on. "Why should I?" replied Joe. "When somebody insulted Caruso, did he sing an aria for him?"

This is one of my favorite illustrations because it is so relevant to the theme of identity. The truck driver clearly didn't know the real identity of the person he was cursing, for if he had, he would have treated him in a dramatically different way! On the other hand, Joe Louis knew who he was—the best boxer in the world—and therefore he had nothing to prove. Many other men in his position would have been tempted to fight back or at least return insult for insult. But Louis was secure enough in his identity to understand that such a response would only be degrading. The truck driver's opinion of him was irrelevant to Joe's self-understanding.

I have come to view this issue of identity as a powerful potential source of motivation for believers, particularly during times of temptation and spiritual warfare.

So far we have looked at rewards, love, gratitude, fear, and the lack of other options as factors that can keep us in the race and move us away from disobedience and toward Christlikeness. Coming to grips with our true identity in Christ can also be a significant component of godly motivation, but lamentably, this rarely seems to be the case. The problem here is that most people who have received God's gift of forgiveness and life in Christ have either forgotten or have never grasped what it means to be a child of God.

Charlie Chaplin entered a Charlie Chaplin look-alike competition in Monte Carlo—he came in third. We too are getting mixed signals about our identity. Our parents, friends, associates, and society give us one set of impressions, and to the extent that we expose ourselves to Scripture, we discover an entirely different picture. The usual way of resolving these conflicting inputs is to filter out the biblical passages that do not fit the self-perception we have picked up from the world. For instance, many of us have experienced significant amounts of performance-based acceptance. Because of this, we may conclude that love is conditional and must be merited. When Scripture tells us that as believers in Christ we are unconditionally loved and accepted by the Father, we find it difficult to internalize since it is so radically opposed to everything the world has told us. When we read in Ephesians 1–2 that we are not only members of God's family, but we are already seated with Christ in the heavenly places, we are inclined to think it must be talking about someone else. When Romans 6 tells us that we have died with Christ and no longer need be dominated by the power of sin, we say that our experience suggests otherwise.

Our culture tells us that our worth is determined by our accomplishments and encourages us to pursue significance and meaning through the things we do. Scripture tells us that our worth is determined by what Christ was willing to do for us, and that in Him we have an unlimited and unchanging source of meaning and purpose. Who we are in Christ is not shaped by what we do, but by what He did on the cross and continues to do in our lives. It is not our performance that determines our identity;

instead, our new identity in Jesus becomes the basis for what we do. If we perceive ourselves to be worthless or inadequate, this will be manifested in our behavior. But if we choose to acknowledge the truth of Scripture, we will begin to see God and ourselves in a new light. In spite of what our culture and experiences have taught us to feel, the New Testament tells us that we became new creatures when we trusted in Christ. In Him, we have been granted great dignity, security, forgiveness, unconditional love and acceptance, hope, purpose, righteousness, wholeness, and peace with God. We may not *feel* that these things are so, but Scripture does not command us to feel the truth but to believe it. This is a matter of acknowledging its authority by taking God at His word in spite of how we feel or who we think we are.

As we expose ourselves to Scripture and make the faith decision to regard its proclamations as true, we are inviting the Holy Spirit to make these truths more real not only in our thinking, but gradually in our feelings as well. This internalization process requires the discipline of mental renewal through time in the Word, of becoming equipped through good teaching, and fellowship with like-minded people in the spiritual journey.

We honor God when we allow Him to define us and tell us who we are regardless of our feelings or experiences to the contrary. In Christ, we are overcomers who have been adopted into God's family; set free from bondage to Satan, sin, and death; called and equipped to accomplish an eternal purpose that will have enduring results; raised up with Christ and partakers of His life; sealed, anointed, indwelled, and empowered by the Holy Spirit; recipients of an imperishable inheritance that is reserved in heaven for us; members of the body of Christ and joint heirs with Him; chosen, redeemed, forgiven, and set apart; destined to be raised in a glorified body in which we will behold God and live in communion with Him forever. Since things are so, and since nothing can separate us from the love of God which is in Christ Jesus our Lord (Romans 8:38–39), we are spiritual champions who are called to live as such. Like Joe Louis, when we know who we are, we have nothing to prove. Furthermore, the degradation of sin is beneath the dignity of the people we have become in Christ. When we are tempted to covet, lust, lie, become envious, or succumb to any other work of the flesh, we should say, "That is no longer who I am." While we are on this earth, the lust of the flesh, the lust of the eye, and the boastful pride of life will be constant snares, but we are more than conquerors when we remember that our deepest identity is in Christ and when we invite Him to rule and live through us.

PURPOSE AND HOPE

In 1902 Meyer Kubelski, a Jewish immigrant from Russia, gave his son a violin for his eighth birthday. It cost Meyer fifty dollars, a small fortune in those days.

The son loved music and soon was playing well enough to give concerts at the Barrison Theater in Waukeegan, the town where the Kubelskis lived. By the age of eighteen, he had teamed up with a woman pianist as a concert team in vaudeville.

One night as Benjamin Kubelski was playing, he felt impelled, between numbers, to tell the audience about a funny incident that had happened to him during the day. "The audience laughed," he recalled later, "and the sound intoxicated me. That laughter ended my days as a musician." Jack Benny, as the young Kubelski later called himself, had found his rightful career.

Most people never stumble, as Benny did, into a career path that so happily meshes ability and passion. But even if the fit is perfect, a career is not the same as a biblical purpose for one's life. Vocational setbacks and retirement do not derail God's purpose for us, because His intentions transcend the circumstances and seasons of our lives. Even marriage and children, as crucial as these are, cannot be equated with God's unchanging reason for our being.

Laying hold of a sense of purpose can be a significant source of motivation, but the problem is that even as believers, we are more inclined to pursue temporal rather than biblical purposes. In fact, most people fail to wrestle with the issue of purpose at all; without thought-out purposes to guide them, they base their decisions instead on activities and objectives that have become ends in themselves.

This is the antithesis of the way the Lord Jesus ordered His earthly life. Jesus had a clear understanding of the purpose of His life, and He derived His purpose from His Father and not His own ambitions or aspirations. The hallmark of His life was to learn His Father's will and walk in the power of the Spirit to bring it to fruition. The gospels record three particularly clear purpose statements that related to our Lord's life mission: "For even the Son of Man did not come to be served, but to serve, and to give His life a ransom for many.... For the Son of Man has come to seek and to save that which was lost.... I glorified You on the earth, having accomplished the work which You have given Me to do" (Mark 10:45; Luke 19:10; John 17:4). Jesus' purpose was to glorify His Father by seeking, serving, and saving the lost.

The apostle Paul also had a well-defined sense of purpose that involved a passion for knowing and pleasing Christ and for remaining faithful to his personal calling to evangelism and edification (see Philippians 3:10, 13–14; 2 Corinthians 5:9; 1 Corinthians 9:24–27; 2 Timothy 4:7–8).

We cannot lay hold of God's unique purpose for our lives without spending time with Him and inviting Him to clarify His purpose for us in His timing and in His way. It is never too late to begin wrestling with the reason for our earthly existence, since God in His sovereignty can use all our previous experiences to prepare us for our true mission. Ask the Lord to give you a personal purpose statement and a passion to fulfill it. (My own personal purpose statement is "to be a lover and servant of God and others.") It is in this way that your activities and objectives will take on a depth of meaning.

Hope is related to purpose since both of these biblical motivators move us in the direction of long-term gain. Some people have no hope; most have a misplaced or an ill-defined hope, and a few have a proper hope. It is not uncommon for those who know Christ to succumb to the error of putting their hope in Him for their eternal destiny and putting their hope in the world for everything else.

When this happens, the pursuit of security, significance, and satisfaction takes precedence over the pursuit of Christ. Ironically, the more we pursue these things for themselves, the more elusive they become. They are only given to us in their fullness as the overflow of seeking first the Lord's kingdom and righteousness.

Hebrews 6:11–20 instructs us to fix our hope solely on the character and promises of the God of Abraham, Isaac, and Jacob. There is but one safe refuge for hope in this world, and that is the unchanging character of the triune God and the certain promises of Scripture that flow out of His character. "This hope we have as an anchor of the soul, a hope both sure and steadfast and one which enters within the veil, where Jesus has entered as a forerunner for us" (Hebrews 6:19–20). Thus, hope in the Bible is *assured by God's character.*

A godly hope is also *achieved through adversity.* We are more likely to come into contact with our hope during times of trial and affliction than during times of success and prosperity, since the latter has a way of knitting our hearts to the promises of this world rather than the promises of the Word. As Paul told the Romans, "We exult in hope of the glory of God. And not only this, but we also exult in our tribulations, knowing that tribulation brings about perseverance; and perseverance, proven character; and proven character, hope; and hope does not disappoint, because the love of God has been poured out within our hearts through the Holy Spirit who was given to us" (Romans 5:2–5). In the same epistle he added, "I consider that the sufferings of this present time are not worthy to be compared with the glory that is to be revealed to us.... For in hope we have been saved, but hope that is seen is not hope; for why does one also hope for what he sees? But if we hope for what we do not see, with perseverance we wait eagerly for it" (8:18, 24–25). Morris Inch *(Psychology in the Psalms)* notes that biblical hope "does not reduce the ingredients of living, but adds God to the equation. Hope shouts, not because there is no enemy, but because God gives the triumph. Hope sings, not because there is no night, but because God gives songs in the night. The pulse of hope is praise."

We lay hold of biblical hope by faith (Ephesians 1:18), and the more it motivates us, the more it becomes evident to others (1 Peter 1:3; 3:15). It also assures us that whatever God calls us to do will be more than worth it all. "Therefore, my beloved brethren, be steadfast, immovable, always abounding in the work of the Lord, knowing that your toil is not in vain in the Lord" (1 Corinthians 15:58).

Motivated Spirituality

WHY DO WE DO WHAT WE DO?
DO WE LONG FOR GOD?

As the deer pants for the water brooks,
so my soul pants for Thee, O God.
My soul thirsts for God, for the living God;
when shall I come and appear before God?
PSALM 42:1–2

As we conclude this portrait of biblical motivators, we approach
the one I believe to be the highest but the least commonly experienced spiritual source of motivation: the longing for God Himself.

Moses' great prayer in the wilderness was "I pray You, show
me Your glory!" (Exodus 33:18); the psalmists cultivated a passion
for God's presence and understood that anything of true value
comes from His hand; the sages who wrote the wisdom literature
stressed that nothing at all can compare with knowing God; the
prophets were overwhelmed with the splendor and majesty of
God and endured ridicule and rejection in order to be pleasing to
Him; Jesus taught His followers to hunger and thirst more for
God's kingdom and righteousness than for anything else; the
apostles' deepest longing was to behold the infinite Lover of their
souls.

Longing to see God and to enter His consummate presence is
an oft-repeated theme in the writings of the great saints in the history of the church, but it is rarely seen in the Christian literature
of this century. In my own experience, I find myself longing to

long for God in the way some of these men and women did. Six
hundred years ago, for instance, Julian of Norwich in her
Revelations of Divine Love asked God for faithful wounds of contrition for her sins, compassion for others, and an intense longing
for God. She wrote, "At the same moment the Trinity filled me
full of heartfelt joy, and I knew that all eternity was like this for
those who attain heaven. For the Trinity is God, and God the
Trinity; the Trinity is our Maker and keeper, our eternal lover, joy
and bliss—all through our Lord Jesus Christ.... We have got to
realize the littleness of creation and to see it for the nothing that it
is before we can love and possess God who is uncreated. This is
the reason why we have no ease of heart or soul, for we are seeking our rest in trivial things which cannot satisfy, and not seeking
to know God, almighty, all-wise, all-good. He is true rest. It is His
will that we should know Him, and His pleasure that we should
rest in Him. Nothing less will satisfy us.... We shall never cease
wanting and longing until we possess Him in fullness and joy.
Then we shall have no further wants. Meanwhile His will is that
we go on knowing and loving until we are perfected in heaven....
The more clearly the soul sees the blessed face by grace and love,
the more it longs to see it in its fullness."

C. S. Lewis in his autobiography, *Surprised by Joy,* related true
joy to what he called *Sehnsucht,* or longing. He spoke of the stab
and pang of acute longing as homesickness for a place and a time
we have not yet visited that is beyond the edge of the imagination.

> The sense that in this universe we are treated as strangers,
> the longing to be acknowledged, to meet with some
> response, to bridge some chasm that yawns between us
> and reality, is part of our inconsolable secret. And surely,
> from this point of view, the promise of glory, in the sense
> described, becomes highly relevant to our deep desire. For
> glory meant good report with God, acceptance by God,
> response, acknowledgment, and welcome into the heart
> of things. The door on which we have been knocking all
> our lives will open at last.... Apparently, then, our lifelong

nostalgia, our longing to be reunited with something in the universe from which we now feel cut off, to be on the inside of some door which we have always seen from the outside, is no mere neurotic fancy, but the truest index of our real situation. And to be at last summoned inside would be both glory and honour beyond all our merits and also the healing of that old ache.

"Things which eye has not seen and ear has not heard, and which have not entered the heart of man, all that God has prepared for those who love Him" (1 Corinthians 2:9).

There have been times when a walk in the woods, a painting, a photograph, or a piece of music created a sudden and profound sense of longing within me. When I thought about it, I realized that in each case, the vehicle that caused the longing pointed not to itself, but to that which is beyond the created order, to God Himself. These are fleeting moments, but they are enough to remind me of the reality of my pilgrim status and to awaken desire for something more than anything this world can offer.

Along similar lines, Henri Nouwen in his perceptive book *The Return of the Prodigal Son,* describes his encounter with Rembrandt's painting of this parable and the remarkable effect the painting had on his self-understanding. "It had brought me into touch with something within me that lies far beyond the ups and downs of a busy life, something that represents the ongoing yearning of the human spirit, the yearning for a final return, an unambiguous sense of safety, a lasting home." It is an aspiration to turn to our Father's house and to find the deep satisfaction of His embrace and of being treasured by Him. "In My Father's house are many dwelling places; if it were not so, I would have told you; for I go and prepare a place for you. And if I go and prepare a place for you, I will come again, and receive you to Myself; that where I am, there you may be also" (John 14:2–3).

Coming to Christ is "not an end but an inception, for now begins the glorious pursuit, the heart's happy exploration of the infinite riches of the Godhead. That is where we begin, I say, but where we stop no man has yet discovered, for there is in the awful and mysterious depths of the Triune God neither limit nor end.... To have found God and still to pursue Him is the soul's paradox of love, scorned indeed by the too-easily-satisfied religionist, but justified in happy experience by the children of the burning heart" (A. W. Tozer, *The Pursuit of God*). This holy desire, this transcendent ambition, is captured in Jesus' penetrating words, "Seek first His kingdom and His righteousness; and all these things shall be added to you" (Matthew 6:32–33). "Jesus took it for granted that all human beings are 'seekers.' It is not natural for people to drift aimlessly through life like plankton. We need something to live for, something to give meaning to our existence, something to 'seek,' something on which to set our hearts and our minds" (John Stott, *Christian Counter-Culture*).

God waits to be wanted, but He must be wanted for Himself and not for some lesser good He may provide. May we ask for the grace to long for the beatific vision, for the vision of God Himself. "There shall no longer be any curse; and the throne of God and of the Lamb shall be in it, and His bond-servants shall serve Him; *and they shall see His face,* and His name shall be on their foreheads" (Revelation 22:3–4).

Epilogue

The introduction, "A Gem with Many Facets," began with a look at the growing awareness of spirituality in our time and the importance of distinguishing biblical and unbiblical approaches to this important subject. After summarizing the twelve facets of Christian spirituality that are discussed in *That I May Know God* and its sequel, *Following Hard after God,* I stressed the need for diversity in light of the fact that no single approach to the spiritual life is exhaustive. In addition, the various types of spirituality resonate to differing degrees with our personalities and temperaments, and this is developed more fully in appendix A. It is important to see why we are attracted to some types of spirituality and not to others, as well as the value of exposure to approaches we would normally ignore or resist.

A brief history of Christian spirituality is covered in appendix B, "The Richness of Our Heritage." This provides an overview of the great diversity of spiritual approaches in the ancient, medieval, and modern church eras, along with an analysis of various extremes relating to twelve recurring issues. I hope that this historical overview will expand your appreciation of this rich and complex subject.

The chapters on relational spirituality explored the riches of God's love as the foundation for our loving response to Him. To know Him is to love Him, and the more we love God, the more we are willing to trust and follow Him. This vertical relationship should define us and become the basis for our self-understanding. As this grows, we become secure enough in Christ to love and serve others.

The chapters on paradigm spirituality developed the critical theme of cultivating and living out an eternal perspective in the context of a temporal arena. This is an ongoing challenge because the claims of the temporal value system are constantly being reinforced in our culture. It is only by focusing our attention on the things that God says are important that we will avoid the tragic error of giving our lives in exchange for trivia.

The chapters on disciplined spirituality outlined the classic spiritual disciplines that have been practiced throughout the history of the church and accented the importance of balancing these disciplines with an ongoing sense of dependence upon God. We considered the benefits of practicing the spiritual disciplines, and after describing twenty of these disciplines, we focused on the key disciplines of solitude and silence, study, meditation, and prayer.

The chapters on exchanged life spirituality looked at God's plan to satisfy our deep spiritual needs so that we would look to Him as our true source of security, significance, and satisfaction. Having trusted in Christ, we must grow in our understanding of the reality of our identification with Him in His death, burial, and resurrection.

The chapters on motivated spirituality examined seven biblically based motivations for staying in the process of walking in trust and obedience to the Lord. Some of these incentives will be more compelling to one believer than another, but all of them are founded in the truths of Scripture.

The sequel to this book, *Following Hard after God*, presents seven more facets of spirituality (devotional, holistic, process, Spirit-filled, warfare, nurturing, and corporate) and deals with the issue of what it takes to keep our focus on Christ so that we finish well.

It is my prayer that you benefit from this exposure to the diversity of approaches that have been used to cultivate spiritual growth and that you explore some of the facets that may have been less familiar to you.

The Lord bless you and keep you;
The Lord make His face shine upon you
And be gracious to you;
The Lord turn His face toward you
And give you peace.
NUMBERS 6:24–26

The Need for Diversity

The facets of spirituality mentioned in the introduction point to the centrality of the Lord Jesus Christ, and each of them adds a unique dimension to the gem of the spiritual life. Thus, it would be a mistake to reduce our understanding of the sanctification process to any one of these approaches, and yet this is commonly done. For instance, a number of writers who stress the truths of the exchanged life virtually ignore the need for the disciplines of the faith or the corporate aspects of spiritual growth. There are others who are so concerned about the reality of spiritual warfare that they overlook the process of integrating our relationship with Christ in the routines of daily living.

When we get excited about the power of the Holy Spirit or corporate worship or the spiritual disciplines or sharing our faith with others in a relational way, it is easy to focus so intently on the insights we have gained in one of these areas that we come to view this single approach as the panacea for spiritual development. This leads to a one-sidedness that when carried too far leaves us vulnerable to the latent weaknesses of any of these approaches. For instance, devotional spirituality left to itself can lead to an individualistic sentimentality, while disciplined spirituality left to itself can lead to an overemphasis on willpower and self-effort. But when these approaches are fit together into a more comprehensive whole, they inform and balance one another. When we view them as complementary components, we are less inclined to think of them as formulas or recipes. Instead, each of the twelve facets is really a symbiotic, divine/human dynamic that requires both dependence *and* discipline. When we reduce these approaches to techniques, we miss the Augustinian truth that we come to God by love and not by navigation. It is essential to acknowledge the primacy of God's grace over determined self-actualization, or we will deceive ourselves into thinking that our efforts and methods are the means of spiritual growth. When we succumb to this illusion, we will try to control God by our formulas and routines.

Even when we acknowledge that there are several legitimate and complementary approaches to growth in the spiritual life, there is a natural tendency to limit ourselves to the one that best fits our personality and to assume that if it works for us, it should work for others. And because of this tendency, many new believers are exposed to only one or two approaches, neither of which may be particularly helpful in view of their temperaments and predispositions. In recent years, these concerns have been addressed by writers who have sought to identify various types of Christian spirituality and to relate these types to differing mental and emotional character traits. For example, Allan H. Sager in *Gospel-Centered Spirituality* adapted a phenomenology of spirituality developed by Urban T. Holmes in his important book *A History of Christian Spirituality.* This typology involves both a horizontal and a vertical continuum. The vertical scale concerns a person's relational orientation to God, and this can range from purely cognitive and speculative illumination of the mind at one end of the spectrum to purely affective and emotional illumination of the heart at the opposite end of the spectrum. The horizontal scale concerns a person's preferred means of pursuing the spiritual life, and this can range from a purely *kataphatic* orientation to a purely *apophatic* orientation. The term *kataphatic* is derived from a Greek word that means affirmative, and this refers to the tradition known as the *via affirmativa,* the way of affirmation. This tradition, more characteristic of the West, stresses the knowledge of God through general and special revelation. The term *apophatic* is derived from a Greek word that means negative, and this speaks of the tradition known as the *via negativa,* the way of negation. This tradition, more characteristic of the East, stresses God's transcendence and mystery. Thus, a kataphatic style of spirituality uses symbols, images, and metaphors while an apophatic style emphasizes God's hiddenness.

In reality, no one is purely cerebral, with no emotion, or solely heart without mind (the vertical scale). Similarly, no believer behaves as if God is utterly hidden or completely knowable (the horizontal scale). Instead, as the Types of Christian Spirituality chart shows, there is a wide range for diversity that incorporates elements from each of the types in manifold ways. Refer to the chart on page 166.

A K+/M+ (high kataphatic/high mind) is very different in orientation and style from an A+/H+ (high apophatic/high heart). There are also differences within each quadrant; for example, within the K/H quadrant, there are nine combinations that range from a K-/H- to a K+/H+.

Apophatic/Heart (A/H) spirituality involves both intuition and feelings, and this combination encourages a diligent pursuit of an inward consciousness of God that stresses prayer and solitude. Theologians of the inner life include Bernard of Clairvaux, Thomas à Kempis, and Cistercian monastics such as Thomas Merton. Taken too far, this form of spirituality can lead to quietism—a neglect of the world and an excessive introspection.

Kataphatic/Mind (K/M) spirituality involves both revelation and understanding, and this combination encourages rational engagement with spiritual truth. Advocates of theological renewal include Thomas Aquinas, Ignatius of Loyola, Martin Luther, John Calvin, and Karl Barth. Taken too far, this form of spirituality can lead to rationalism—an overly dogmatic emphasis that stresses logic to the exclusion of mystery and propositional truth over personal response.

Kataphatic/Heart (K/H) spirituality involves both revelation and feelings, and this combination encourages outward expression of inner change and transformation of society one life at a time. Proponents of personal renewal include St. Benedict, several

TYPES OF CHRISTIAN SPIRITUALITY

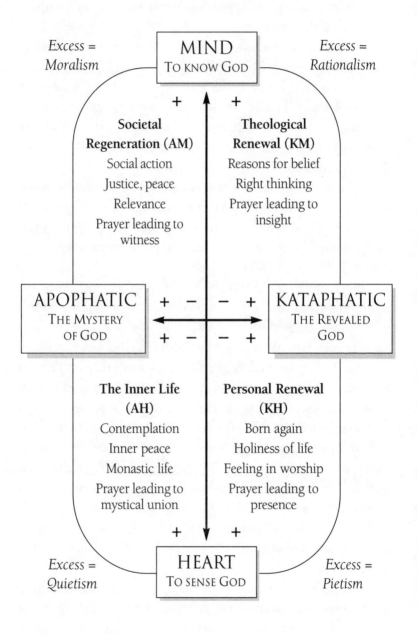

Excess =
Moralism

MIND
TO KNOW GOD

Excess =
Rationalism

+   +

**Societal
Regeneration (AM)**

Social action
Justice, peace
Relevance
Prayer leading to
witness

**Theological
Renewal (KM)**

Reasons for belief
Right thinking
Prayer leading to
insight

APOPHATIC
THE MYSTERY
OF GOD

+   −   −   +

+   −   −   +

KATAPHATIC
THE REVEALED
GOD

**The Inner Life
(AH)**

Contemplation
Inner peace
Monastic life
Prayer leading to
mystical union

**Personal Renewal
(KH)**

Born again
Holiness of life
Feeling in worship
Prayer leading to
presence

+   +

Excess =
Quietism

HEART
TO SENSE GOD

Excess =
Pietism

*Based on "A Circle of Sensibility" from *A History of Christian Spirituality* © 1980 by Urban Holmes III. Used by permission.

Puritan writers, Charles Wesley, and many modern evangelicals. Taken too far, this form of spirituality can lead to pietism—an excessive emotionalism, experientialism, and an anti-intellectualism.

Apophatic/Mind (A/M) spirituality involves both intuition and understanding, and this combination encourages bold action and a concern for social justice. Champions of societal regeneration include the prophet Amos, Francis of Assisi, Albert Schweitzer, and Martin Luther King Jr. Taken too far, this form of spirituality can lead to moralism—a mind-set of cultural condemnation and an excessive emphasis on action over being.

Using the twelve facets of spirituality that are presented in *That I May Know God* and *Following Hard after God*, we can draw a *very general* correlation between these facets and the four types of spirituality we have just discussed:

Clearly, these generalizations admit many exceptions, since

APOPHATIC/MIND	KATAPHATIC/MIND
◆ Corporate Spirituality	◆ Paradigm Spirituality
◆ Holistic Spirituality	◆ Motivated Spirituality
◆ Warfare Spirituality	◆ Nurturing Spirituality
APOPHATIC/HEART	**KATAPHATIC/HEART**
◆ Devotional Spirituality	◆ Relational Spirituality
◆ Disciplined Spirituality	◆ Exchanged Life Spirituality
◆ Process Spirituality	◆ Spirit-filled Spirituality

there are aspects of each of the twelve facets that relate to each of the four quadrants above. But it is helpful to note, for example, that people with a K/H bent are far more likely to be drawn to exchanged life or Spirit-filled spirituality than they will be to corporate spirituality or an emphasis on social justice that is more characteristic of those with an A/M orientation.

A different, but equally helpful typology of spiritual orientations can be derived from the Myers-Briggs Type Indicator

(MBTI). This preference indicator was adapted by Katharine Briggs and Isabel Myers from Carl G. Jung's personality classifications in his book on psychological types. (In recent years, Jung has become quite popular in Christian as well as New Age circles, and the use of his ideas by Christian writers and counselors requires more discernment than is often practiced. Jung's preoccupation with the movement toward wholeness and individuation and his fascination with mandalas, Eastern mysticism, alchemy, and occultism led to the development of a speculative, complex, and esoteric psychological theory with unavoidably metaphysical overtones. Unlike most personality theorists, Jung explicitly recognized the importance of spiritual concerns, but his attempt to resurrect spiritual symbolism that is devoid of creedal content led him to an amalgam of psychology and spirituality that approximates a rival religion that replaces dogma with the contents of the unconscious. Jung spurned the idea of God as an objective transcendent reality and turned instead to primal symbols stripped of their transcendent referents. Thus, the use of Jung's typology in this chapter is not an endorsement of his system of thought.)

The MBTI uses four pairs of preferences, and each of these pairs forms a continuum:

1. The extraversion/introversion (E/I) scale concerns a person's relative preference for being energized by the outer world of people and things versus the inner world of ideas. Extraverts are active, outgoing, participative, open, and verbal thinkers. Introverts are reflective, inwardly directed, reserved, and mental thinkers.

2. The sensing/intuition (S/N) scale concerns one's relative preference for perceiving and processing information through known facts versus possibilities and relationships. Sensors are oriented toward tangible sensory data, details, and present reality. Intuitives are oriented toward abstract idealistic associations, future possibilities, and theoretical patterns.

3. The thinking/feeling (T/F) preference concerns the way people arrive at conclusions. Thinkers base their judgments more on impersonal, objective analysis and are concerned with justice,

truth, and logic. Feelers base their judgments more on personal, subjective values and are concerned with harmony, tact, and humane treatment.

4. The judging/perceiving (J/P) scale concerns people's preferential orientation to outer life. Judgers are more inclined toward a systematic, organized, and planned lifestyle that involves goals, deadlines, and controlled procedures. Perceivers are more inclined toward a flexible and spontaneous lifestyle that welcomes change, surprise, and open-ended approaches.

When these four preferential pairs are combined, they result in sixteen basic personality types ranging from ESTJ to INFP. But there are many nuances within each of these personality types, since each pair constitutes a continuum that can range, for example, from a strong E to a borderline E or I to a strong I. Thus, this typology allows for the uniqueness of each individual while offering insights into the way people can be grouped according to preferential patterns. (It should be noted that there is no hint of superiority or inferiority in these patterns, since they are based on personal preferences. Additional factors such as intelligence, abilities, skills, drive, and maturity add an enormous number of personality nuances.)

Those who follow Christ tend to gravitate toward the spiritual activities that nurture their preferential patterns. Up to a point, this is healthy since it provides great diversity within the unity of the body of Christ. But as M. Robert Mulholland Jr. observes in *Invitation to a Journey,* each of the four preferential pairs, when carried to either extreme (e.g., all T and no F or all F and no T) can lead to a spiritually unhealthy one-sidedness. For instance, when extraversion is carried too far, it can result in such an emphasis on the social dynamics of the spiritual life that there is no room for the depth that solitude and reflection can provide. Strong introverts, on the other hand, can avoid community and practice spiritual isolation. Similarly, strong thinkers can be too prone to a highly analytical and systematic approach to the spiritual life, while strong feelers can be vulnerable to sentimentality, emotionalism, and the quest for repeated experiential authentication.

Earle C. Page, in connection with the Center for Applications of Psychological Type, has developed two helpful charts that illustrate several connections between the MBTI preferences and one's spiritual orientation. The first of these, "Finding Your Spiritual Path," is a useful diagnostic tool *see* page 171).

The second chart *see* page 172), "Following Your Spiritual Path," points to the positive and negative spiritual expressions that are associated with the four preference pairs.

Several authors relate these personality styles to the practice of spirituality and to distinctive approaches to prayer. In the following chart, I have summarized the prayer typology developed by Charles J. Keating in his book *Who We Are Is How We Pray.*

THE INTROVERTED PERSONALITY	Prayer within ourselves–complex, non-conforming, personal
THE EXTRAVERTED PERSONALITY	Open prayer–outward orientation, communal
THE INTUITIVE PERSONALITY	Prayer of hope—possibilities, spiritual communion, reflection
THE SENSING PERSONALITY	Practical prayer—contact with environment, present orientation
THE FEELING PERSONALITY	Feeling prayer—emotional dynamics, personal integration
THE THINKING PERSONALITY	Prayer of reason—rationally ordered and logical approach, truth orientation
THE JUDGING PERSONALITY	Orderly prayer—little ambiguity, structural orientation
THE PERCEIVING PERSONALITY	Lived prayer—accepts ambiguity, several approaches, enthusiastic

Finding Your Spiritual Path

Note: These words are meant to suggest, not to define or to limit understanding.

Preferred Attitude, Function, or Lifestyle	EXTRAVERSION E	INTROVERSION I	SENSING S	INTUITION N	THINKING T	FEELING F	JUDGEMENT J	PERCEPTION P
Primary Arena	World/Other	Ideas/Self	Body	Spirit	Mind	Heart	Will	Awareness
Preference for	Action	Reflection	Sensory reality Details Status quo	Possibilities Patterns Change	Objective values	Subjective values	Initiative	Response
Significant Aspects of Reality	Exterior	Interior	Immediacy Concreteness	Anticipation Vision	Theory Principles	Feeling, Memory, Ideal	Product Categorical	Process Conditional
Windows through which God's Revelation is Received	People Events Scripture Natural world	Individual Experience Inspiration Inner world	Society Institutions "The Seen"	Insight Imagination "The Unseen"	Reason Speculation	Relationships Emotions	Order "Ought"	Serendipity "Is"
Significant Aspects of God	Immanence Creator Imago Dei	Transcendence Identity of God and inner self	Incarnation	Mystery Holy Spirit	The Absolute Principle First Cause	Relational Familial (e.g. Father)	Judge Ruler	Redeemer Healer
Approach to Bible, Religious Experience	Social	Solitary	Practical Literal	Symbolic Metaphorical	Analytical Abstract	Personal Immediate	Systematic	Of-the-Moment
Avoids (Hell)	Exclusion Loneliness	Intrusions Confusion	Ambiguity	Restriction Repetition	Inconsistency Ignorance	Conflict Estrangement	Helplessness Disorder	Regimentation Deadlines
Seeks (Heaven)	Participation Reunion	Incorporation Fulfillment	Physical harmony Faithfulness Obedience	Aesthetic harmony Mystical union	Conceptual harmony Enlightenment Justice, Truth	Personal harmony Communion Appreciation	Closure Productivity Work ethic	Openness Receptivity Play ethic
Prayer	Corporate	Private	Sensuous (eyes, ears, nose, hands, mouth)	Intuitive	Cognitive	Affective	Planned	Unplanned
Natural Spiritual Path	Action	Reflection	Service	Awareness	Knowledge	Devotion	Discipline	Spontaneity
Needed for Wholeness	Reflection	Action or Participation	Awareness or Understanding	Service or Embodiment	Devotion	Knowledge	Spontaneity	Discipline

Following Your Spiritual Path

Note: Our aim is a balanced, centered spirituality. These words are meant to facilitate understanding, not to stifle individuality.

SPIRITUAL PATH	ACTION E	REFLECTION I	SERVICE S	AWARENESS N	KNOWLEDGE T	DEVOTION F	DISCIPLINE J	SPONTANEITY P
Some Positive Expressions	Assertiveness Building community	Independence Deepening community	Love Pleasure	Ecstasy Anticipation	Equanimity Objectivity	Compassion Rapport, Trust	Discrimination Competence	Acceptance Serenity
Some Negative Expressions	Anger Attack	Fear Withdrawal	Attachment	Elation Depression	Apathy Criticalness	Sentimentality Overprotectiveness	Inappropriate control Judging others	Failure to take responsibility
UnderDevelopment May Lead to	Isolation Lack of circumspection	Emptiness Dependence	Abstraction Overlooking	Flatness	Confusion	Coldness Distrust	Loss of purpose Indecision	Premature closure Baseless conclusions
OverDevelopment May Lead to	Impatience Shallowness	Withholding Idiosyncrasy Inappropriate intensity	Idolatry Frivolity Inappropriate conformity	Illusion Impracticality Stubbornness Fickleness	Reductionism Cynicism Dogmatism Rumination	Credulity Personalizing Blaming	Rigidity Perfectionism	Passivity Impulsiveness Procrastination
Special Temptations and Vulnerabilities	Distraction Suggestibility	Inaction Inclusion by others	Superstition Suspicion Fear of change	Primitive sensuality Psychogenic illness	Emotional explosion, exploitation, indulgence Contaminated thinking	Idealizing authority Pseudo-objectivity Hurt feelings	Self-righteousness Scrupulosity	Rebelliousness Carelessness
Needed for Wholeness	Reflection	Action or Participation	Awareness	Service or Embodiment	Devotion	Knowledge	Spontaneity	Discipline

Combining Keating and other sources, here is a distillation of the sixteen personality types in terms of spiritual orientation and prayer:

I S T J INTROVERTED SENSING WITH THINKING	I S F J INTROVERTED SENSING WITH FEELING
• Serious, quiet, thorough, orderly, logical, private • Sense of responsibility • Private spirituality • Enjoys scheduled and consistent prayer • Conscience orientation; will of God	• Dependable, conservative, strong sense of duty, often taken for granted • Desires to please God • Attracted to orderly spiritual regimen • Silent, private prayer • Community orientation; present expression of spirituality
I S T P INTROVERTED THINKING WITH SENSING	I S F P INTROVERTED FEELING WITH SENSING
• Practical, precise, reserved, objective • Action over prayer; practice of the presence of God • Individual approach to prayer and spiritual growth • Needs time for private meditation • Thinking and concentration, but needs practical application	• Free spirit, impulsive, intense feelings, artistic, appreciation for life • Open to social dimensions of personal spirituality • Flexible prayer forms; needs the discipline of private reflection • Present-tense experiential orientation
E S T P EXTRAVERTED SENSING WITH THINKING	E S F P EXTRAVERTED SENSING WITH FEELING
• Action-oriented; pragmatic, realistic, unpredictable, flexible • Experiences of community, praise, singing • Requires minimal spiritual structure • Spontaneous prayers • Communal theological orientation	• Charismatic, attractive personalities • Lives primarily for the moment • People-oriented spirituality • Attracted to religious externals • Generous servants, accepting of others • Community orientation

E S T J ExtravertedThinking with Sensing	E S F J Extraverted Feeling with Sensing
• Responsible, orderly, administrative skills, realistic, conservative • Organized approach to spiritual growth, consistent • Institutional spirituality • Practical theological orientation	• Highly sociable, friendly, sympathetic, sentimental, caring • Attracted to prayer groups • Intercessory prayers • Practical application of spirituality • Attracted to experiential mysticism
I N F J Introverted Intuition with Feeling	I N T J Introverted Intuition with Thinking
• Gentle, compassionate, accepting, inspirational; can be stubborn • Not attracted to formal or repetitive prayer • Need for silence; contemplative and conversational prayer • Spiritually reflective on daily events • Mystical orientation	• Self-confident, decisive, pragmatic, single-minded, independent • High achiever; controlling, determined, logically oriented • Attracted to new insights, ideas, inspirations, improvements • Introspective prayer life • Needs time for spiritual reflection
I N F P Introverted Feeling with Intuition	I N T P Introverted Thinking with Intuition
• Idealistic, subjective interpretation; noble service for the benfit of others • Solitary and silent prayer • Personal, spontaneous response to God • Spiritual reflection on daily activities • Desires human support of spiritual development	• Good memory, intelligent, power of concentration, problem solver • Prefers to pray alone; logical, coherent prayer form • Needs space for concentration and evaluation of spiritual insights • Attracted to theological concepts; appraiser of new spiritual insights

E N F P EXTRAVERTED INTUITION WITH FEELING	E N T P EXTRAVERTED INTUITION WITH THINKING
• Optimistic, enthusiastic, imaginative, highly intuitive, skilled with people • Needs significant time for prayerful reflection • Spontaneous, unstructured prayer • Not institutionally motivated • People-oriented spirituality; able to deal with different people and events	• Ingenious, open to new possibilities, resourceful, enthusiastic, innovative • Enjoys novelty, originality, and new forms of prayer • Spontaneous, improvised prayers • Not inclined to a spiritual regimen • Attracted to spiritual conversations with others
E N F J EXTRAVERTED FEELING WITH INTUITION	I N T J EXTRAVERTED THINKING WITH INTUITION
• Motivates people, persuasive, natural leader • Comfortable with many types of prayer; needs time for reflection • Dislikes repetition and routine • People-centered spiritual orientation	• Effective leader, seeks power and competency, outgoing organizer • Theological spirituality • Needs experiences of community • Attracted to structured, logical, consistent prayer forms

Books like *Type Talk* (Otto Kroeger and Janet M. Thuesen), *Please Understand Me* (David Kiersey and Marilyn Bates), and *Life Types* (Sandra Hirsh and Jean Kummerow) are profitable resources for discerning and understanding your personality type. With this information, you can see why you may be attracted to a particular approach to the spiritual life while a spouse or a friend may be uninterested in this approach, but drawn to another. The first two of these books take the sixteen types and divide them into four basic temperaments:

THE SJ TEMPERAMENT	THE SP TEMPERAMENT
ESTJ, ISTJ, ESFJ, ISFJ	ESFP, ISFP, ESTP, ISTP
THE NF TEMPERAMENT	THE NT TEMPERAMENT
ENFJ, INFJ, ENFP, INFP	ENTJ, INTJ, ENTP, INTP

These four temperaments are broader generalizations than the sixteen types, but they are valuable tools for distinguishing fundamental styles of spirituality, as Chester P. Michael and Marie C. Norrisey demonstrate in their book *Prayer and Temperament.* Michael and Norrisey associate four key spiritual leaders in the history of the church with these four temperaments: Ignatius of Loyola (SJ), Francis of Assisi (SP), Thomas Aquinas (NT), and Augustine of Hippo (NF). (The brief history of Christian spirituality in appendix B contextualizeS these and other figures.) In the chart on page 177, I have attempted to illuminate the characteristics of the four temperaments and relate them to the spiritual dimension.

While there seems to be a broad correspondence between these four temperaments and the Performax Personal Profile System (DISC), I must stress that because of the uniqueness of each individual, there are many exceptions. For instance, a person with an NT temperament can be a high D (dominance) instead of a high C (compliance). It is also important to remember that no person is all one temperament, since each of us displays unique combinations and degrees of these personality qualities. But ideally, the personal and spiritual maturation process should move us in the direction of becoming a blended synthesis of all four temperaments, so that we can adapt to people and situations in increasingly flexible and appropriate ways.

As before, using the twelve facets of spirituality that will be presented in *That I May Know God* and *Following Hard after God,* we can draw a *very general* correlation between the twelve facets and these four temperaments (see chart on page 178).

THE SJ TEMPERAMENT	THE SP TEMPERAMENT
◆ James	◆ Peter
◆ Duty	◆ Action
◆ Gospel of Matthew	◆ Gospel of Mark
◆ Ignatian spirituality	◆ Franciscan spirituality
◆ God as one	◆ God as beautiful
◆ Prayer style: structured; use of sensible imagination	◆ Prayer style: informal, spontaneous, brief, practical
◆ About 38% of the U.S. population	◆ About 38% of the U.S. population
◆ *Epimethean* (practical, conservative, obligation, work ethic, history)	◆ *Dionysian* (free spirit, impulsive, initiative, active, *carpe diem*)
◆ Traditional (past orientation)	◆ Adventurous (present orientation)
◆ Economic/commerce	◆ Aesthetic/artistry
◆ D (dominance)	◆ I (influencing)
◆ Motivated by results	◆ Motivated by recognition
◆ Under pressure: autocratic	◆ Under pressure: antagonistic
◆ Task-initiator	◆ Relational-initiator
◆ Choleric	◆ Sanguine

THE NF TEMPERAMENT	THE NT TEMPERAMENT
◆ Paul	◆ John
◆ Vision	◆ Ideas
◆ Gospel of Luke	◆ Gospel of John
◆ Augustinian Spirituality	◆ Thomistic spirituality
◆ God as good	◆ God as true
◆ Prayer style: meditative; use of creative imagination	◆ Prayer style: discursive reflection, directed change
◆ About 12% of the U.S. population	◆ About 12% of the U.S. population
◆ *Apollonian* (personal authentication, verbal creativity, literary skill)	◆ *Promethean* (intelligence, power, competence, understanding)
◆ Idealistic (future orientation)	◆ Inventive (possibility orientation)
◆ Religiosity/ethics	◆ Theoretical/science
◆ S (steadiness)	◆ C (compliance)
◆ Motivated by relationships	◆ Motivated by being right
◆ Under pressure: agreeable	◆ Under pressure: avoidance
◆ Relational-responder	◆ Task-responder
◆ Phlegmatic	◆ Melancholic

THE SJ TEMPERAMENT	THE SP TEMPERAMENT
◆ Disciplined Spirituality ◆ Motivated Spirituality ◆ Holistic Spirituality	◆ Corporate Spirituality ◆ Spirit-filled Spirituality ◆ Warfare Spirituality
THE NF TEMPERAMENT	THE NT TEMPERAMENT
◆ Relational Spirituality ◆ Devotional Spirituality ◆ Exchanged Life Spirituality	◆ Paradigm Spirituality ◆ Process Spirituality ◆ Nurturing Spirituality

It is important to appreciate and affirm your temperamental predisposition regarding spirituality and prayer so that you avoid the discouragement of thinking you must be unspiritual if you don't follow a prescription that works well for someone else. For instance, it can be very liberating for SPs to realize that as spontaneous and informal people, they will not be naturally attracted to the more structured SJ approaches to prayer and spiritual growth. Similarly, as conceptually oriented people, NTs are less inclined to corporate spirituality and Spirit-filled spirituality than are SPs.

At the same time, it is wise and spiritually healthy to identify your opposite preference, type, and temperament and to engage in the discipline of stretching yourself by trying an approach you would not normally pursue. Deliberate participation in a style or facet of spirituality that you are ordinarily inclined to avoid can be a significant source of spiritual growth and greater balance. Using the four preference pairs, for example, it is easy to see that if we are left to ourselves, we would gravitate away from the "shadow" side of our preference pattern. Thus, extraverts would tend to avoid contemplation and solitude, while introverts would tend to avoid social engagement in the spiritual community. Intuitives would tend to avoid the balance and realism of sensory input, while sensors would tend to avoid the value of contemplative and reflective aspects of spirituality. Thinkers would tend to avoid the affective and emotional side of the spiritual life, while feelers would tend to avoid the conceptual and rational aspects of the faith. Judgers would tend to avoid a spontaneous openness to the work of the Spirit, while perceivers would tend to avoid the benefits of the planned and structured side of spirituality.

As an exercise, consider where you think you best fit in regard to the four preference pairs, the sixteen types, and the four temperaments. Then select an approach to spirituality or prayer that would draw you to a greater depth and balance by forcing you to stretch yourself in new and unfamiliar territory. The more you accept the need for this dynamic tension between affirming your natural dispositions and engaging in less preferred ways of being and doing, the more full-orbed and Christlike you will become in your spiritual journey. The Lord Jesus enjoyed the richness of a mystical union with His heavenly Father, but coupled this profound personal experience with social passion and engagement.

In *Rediscovering Holiness,* J. I. Packer addresses the problem of "rhapsody without realism" and "rule-keeping without relating," and argues that all of us, regardless of temperament and natural aptitude, need a healthy balance of doctrine, experience, and practice. We should ask God for the grace to give us the desire and power to choose this biblical combination of knowing, being, and doing.

The Richness of Our Heritage

A BROADER PERSPECTIVE

Most Protestants approach church history and spiritual formation as though nothing of significance occurred between the closing of the New Testament canon in the first century and the Protestant Reformation in the sixteenth century. And even then, there are typically only a few brief pauses along the way to acknowledge the likes of Luther, Calvin, Wesley, Edwards, Whitefield, Spurgeon, and Moody before racing into our own time. Moreover, only a small percentage of contemporary Christians are serious readers (I'm happy you are one of them), and of these, only a meager fraction (I hope you are one of them) expose themselves to the great spiritual writers of previous centuries. As a result, most believers are impoverished by a parochial perspective and are unable to glean from the rich legacy that has been left to us by the followers of the Way since the birth of the church.

This appendix attempts to enhance your exposure to some of the key people and movements that have contributed to our spiritual heritage so that you will have a broader perspective and a sense of continuity with others who have pursued intimacy with God in previous centuries. I will highlight the impressive variety of approaches to Christian discipleship over time and geography, and the following pages will touch on the strengths and weaknesses of some of these styles of spirituality. This process can stretch our awareness, challenge some of our assumptions, and encourage us to explore other facets of the spiritual life.

As inheritors of the extraordinary array of Christian spirituality produced by twenty centuries of development, we have a greater wealth of resources at our disposal than any previous generation. In view of this, it is ironic that there seems to be an unprecedented shallowness and attachment to the current cultural agenda in many of our churches. The emphasis on management models, techniques from pop psychology, and programmatic relevance has led to more interest in buildings, budgets, and body counts than in relational discipleship and spiritual formation. But there are hopeful signs that there is disenchantment with the status quo as increasing numbers of believers look for greater depth and rootedness in true spirituality.

It was only in the last two centuries that Roman Catholic theologians distinguished "mystical theology" or "spirituality" from doctrine as a specialized field. As we will see, however, there is an integral relationship between theology and application; unbiblical and unbalanced doctrines lead to practical distortions. Still, there is prodigious room within the boundaries of theological orthodoxy for a surprising variety of spiritual expressions.

ANCIENT, MEDIEVAL, AND MODERN SPIRITUALITY: A PREVIEW

Church historians have long noted that the combination of the ancient, medieval, and modern periods in the history of the church is shaped like an hourglass. The ancient church (Pentecost to c. 600) was characterized by rapid expansion to the continents of Asia, Africa, and Europe. The medieval church (c. 600 to c. 1500) was marked by withdrawal as internal divisions and the rise of Islam greatly diminished the Christian influence in Asia and Africa. The modern church (c. 1500 to the present) saw a new expansion beyond the boundaries of Europe, and in the past few decades the churches of the third world have shown the greatest vitality, expansion, and missionary fervor.

The ancient church, after it became the official religion of the Roman Empire, was rapidly transformed from a network of periodically persecuted believers into a politically and financially powerful institution. Local churches were organized under regional bishops, and these bishops convened churchwide councils to debate and clarify doctrinal and practical matters. While some of the church fathers dealt with various heresies such as Montanism, Gnosticism, and Neoplatonism, others developed increasingly ascetic lifestyles and left the local churches to pursue a desert spirituality. These desert hermits and monks developed a mystical approach to spiritual formation that was combined with ascetic practices in the growing monastic communities. The three spiritual stages of purgation, illumination, and union were developed and practiced among members of the monastic orders.

Christianity became a predominantly European phenomenon in the Middle Ages, and the Western and Eastern branches of the church formally separated during this period. The spirituality of the Eastern Church became increasingly apophatic and *hesychastic* (the practice of stillness and mystical prayer). Monasticism flourished in the medieval Western Church, and the Benedictine, Carthusian, and Cistercian orders continued to develop a contemplative approach to spirituality. New mendicant orders like the Dominicans and Franciscans were formed, and the rise of scholasticism was paralleled by a rise in a spirituality of service and sacrifice. Mysticism reached its zenith on the European continent and in England in the latter part of the Middle Ages, and the remarkable writings of these Continental and English mystics explored the inner terrain of the soul's journey toward God.

The section on "Spirituality in the Modern Church" in this appendix begins with the impact of the four branches of the Protestant Reformation and touches on Lutheran, Reformed, Anabaptist, and Anglican spirituality. In the Catholic Church, significant spiritual figures arose in sixteenth-century Spain and in seventeenth- and eighteenth-century France. An outline of the varied spiritualities of a number of post-Reformation Protestant movements (Puritans, Quakers, Pietists, Evangelicals, revivalists, Methodists, holiness groups, and Pentecostals) is followed by several recent spiritual figures. This section concludes with a number of recent developments (Vatican II, the ecumenical movement, the charismatic movement, twelve-step spirituality, psychological approaches, and "creation-centered" spirituality), and a word on modern Orthodoxy and spiritual developments in Latin America, Africa, and Asia.

As we consider the history of Christian spirituality during the ancient, medieval, and modern periods, I must stress that this is only a highly selective thumbnail sketch in outline form. There are many books (such as *The Study of Spirituality,* edited by Cheslyn Jones, Geoffrey Wainwright, and Edward Yarnold, SJ; *Handbook of Christian Spirituality* by Michael Cox; the three-volume *A History of Christian Spirituality* by Louis Bouyer; *A History of Christian Spirituality* by Urban T. Holmes; and *Thirsty for God* by Bradley P. Holt) that explore this rich subject in far more detail.

SPIRITUALITY IN THE ANCIENT CHURCH

The Biblical Foundation. The entire Bible points to Jesus Christ as the decisive revelation of God in human history. His redemptive work is the basis for overcoming the fall with its four alienations between people and God, themselves, others, and the created order. A full-orbed biblical spirituality addresses the substantial healing available in Christ in these four areas and anticipates the complete harmony that will come with the new heaven and earth. Jesus' Upper Room Discourse (John 13–17) outlines the essential components of the spiritual life, and the epistles (e.g., Romans 6–8) further develop the meaning of "you in Me, and I in you" (John 14:20).

The Early and Later Patristics (Church Fathers). The church quickly changed from a Messianic sect within Judaism to a pre-dominantly Gentile movement that experienced frequent perse-cution until 313 when Constantine declared Christianity to be a legitimate religion in the Roman Empire. As the church fathers debated and clarified the doctrines of the Trinity and the person and work of Christ, the church as a whole was being consolidated into an institution with growing political and financial power.

Early Christian Worship. The earliest churches adapted the elements of prayer, singing of psalms, reading of Scripture, teaching, and preaching that were used in synagogue worship. There was an emphasis on the use of the charisms, or spiritual gifts, in the earliest assemblies, but this declined by the second century.

The Didache. The *Didache,* or *Teaching of the Twelve Apostles,* reveals the rapid development of structure and hierarchical organization in the second century church.

The Montanists. The followers of Montanus, an influential second century leader in Asia Minor, stressed the imminence of Christ's *Parousia,* or return, and were criticized for charismatic excesses and doctrinal aberrations.

The Martyrs. Because of the persecution of the church in the second and third centuries, the theme of martyrdom was developed as an expression of ultimate commitment to Christ. Ignatius, Bishop of Antioch (c. 35–c. 107), addressed epistles to several churches on his way to martyrdom in the Colosseum during the reign of the Emperor Trajan. Many women were also martyred, such as Perpetua who died for her faith in Carthage around 200.

Gnosticism. The church was plagued by Gnostic heretics who attributed the creation of the material world to an inferior deity (the demiurge) and denied that absolute spirit could ever be incarnated. This led to the twin extremes of asceticism and antinomianism and an emphasis on attaining salvation through hidden knowledge (*gnosis*). The second-century writers Justin Martyr, Irenaeus, and Tertullian refuted the heresy of Gnosticism in their writings.

Asceticism. The spiritual practice of asceticism took two forms in the early church. The unhealthy form denied the goodness of creation and replaced the grace of God with human effort. The healthier form avoided these problems and engaged in self-discipline rather than self-punishment. Tertullian (c. 160–c. 225), a Latin church father who was gifted in doctrinal theology, was excessively rigorous in his ascetic practice of separation from the world.

Hellenistic Influences. Origen of Alexandria (c. 185–284) was thoroughly steeped in Greek philosophy and profoundly affected the church for centuries to come with his allegorical interpretation of Scripture. He and others after him were influenced by the developing Neoplatonism of the time (his contemporary Plotinus, the key Neoplatonist philosopher, taught that the ruling goal of life is union with the Absolute, or One). Origen adapted this philosophy into three spiritual levels of development in the soul's journey to God. The moral level corresponds to Proverbs and relates to behavior; the natural level corresponds to Ecclesiastes and relates to intellectual development; and the contemplative level corresponds to the Song of Songs and relates to spiritual union with God (Origen's allegorical interpretation of the Song of Songs would be used by spiritual writers for centuries to come).

Mysticism. By the fourth century, mysticism became a dominant theme in Christian spirituality. Like the term, *asceticism,* the word *mysticism* can refer to both healthy and unbiblical spiritual practices. In its more biblical sense, mysticism refers to a personal apprehension of the transcendent and ultimate Being. This experience of the presence of God transforms and gives meaning to the created order. By contrast, unbiblical forms of mysticism include oneness mysticism in which the mystic seeks complete absorption and loss of identity in God, and nature mysticism in which the mystic seeks oneness with all things. The word *union* can relate to either the theistic or pantheistic forms of mysticism, while the word *communion* refers to a loving I/Thou relationship between two persons and affirms the Creator/creation distinction. Discernment is required here, since some Christian mystics mean communion when they write of union, while others do not.

Desert Spirituality. Beginning in the third century, a number of men and women entered the deserts of Egypt to live solitary and ascetical lives in the quest for greater intimacy with God. Antony (c. 251–356), described in Athanasius's *Life of Antony,* was the most famous of these early desert hermits, and some of these monks and nuns practiced extreme and bizarre ascetical methods. Anchorites (hermits) also lived in the Syrian desert, and among these were pillar-hermits like Simeon the Elder and Daniel Stylites who lived for decades on small platforms on top of pillars. Ephrem (c. 306–373), another ascetic whose symbolic poetic writings were copied by Syrian monks, influenced Eastern Christianity with his view of the spiritual life as a progression toward *theosis,* or divinization. This concept, based on the 2 Peter 1:4 imagery of becoming "partakers of the divine nature," became a fundamental theme in the spirituality of the Eastern Church.

Monastic Spirituality. Pachomius (c. 290–346) organized a number of desert monasteries and convents, and many of the desert fathers and mothers were associated with these monastic communities, while others lived as solitaries. John Cassian (c. 360–435), a pupil of John Chrysostom, went to Egypt to study desert monasticism, and there he was exposed to the teachings of Evagrius of Pontus (c. 345–399). Evagrius was a Christian Platonist who taught that there are three stages in life (the practical, the natural, and the theological). In his *Institutes* and *Conferences,* John Cassian brought the teachings of Evagrius and other desert monastics to the West where they had an impact on Benedictine monasticism.

Benedict (c. 480–547), founder of the Benedictine Order, developed a system of monastic governance through a *Rule* that provided for *ora et labora,* a combination of prayer and physical labor. The Benedictine *Rule* influenced the entire Western monastic system, as did Benedict's prescription of daily *lectio divina,* or sacred reading.

In the East, Evagrius knew the Cappadocian fathers Basil of Caesarea (c. 330–379), Basil's brother Gregory of Nyssa (c. 330–c. 395), and their friend Gregory of Nazianzus (320–389). Basil of Caesarea wrote two monastic rules that stressed obedience as opposed to self-will, thanksgiving for all things, and the spiritual process of restoring the divine image. Gregory of Nyssa developed a mystical doctrine of ascent that involves a progressive movement into the darkness of growing realization of the incomprehensibility of God.

Augustine. Augustine of Hippo (354–430), the greatest of the Latin fathers, sought to reconcile a personal relationship with God with a strong respect for the authority of the church. As a thinker, he blended a keen intelligence with a powerful intuition;

as a practitioner, he combined a contemplative way of living with a life that was active in the world. His *Confessions* broke new ground with an autobiographical narrative of his developing spiritual life. Augustine's inward journey was driven by an intense longing for God ("You have made us for Yourself, and our heart is restless, until it rests in You") that was increasingly satisfied in his trinitarian reflections and occasional mystical experiences.

Pseudo-Dionysius. A mystical theologian (probably a Syrian monk) who flourished circa 500 penned four books in Greek under the pseudonym Dionysius the Areopagite (Acts 17:34). The writings of Pseudo-Dionysius, as he has come to be known, are *The Divine Names, The Mystical Theology, The Celestial Hierarchy, The Ecclesiastical Hierarchy,* and a collection of letters. These writings were influenced by Neo-Platonism and in turn exerted a powerful influence on Eastern and Western Christian spirituality, particularly in their description of the three spiritual stages. In the *purgative* stage, the soul is cleansed; in the *illuminative* stage, the soul receives the light of God; and in the *unitive* stage, the soul experiences oneness with God. Pseudo-Dionysius was also influential in the development of apophatic theology. He followed the *via negativa,* or the negative way of stripping away intellectual images and attributions of God, and argued that the kataphatic approach was of utility only for spiritual beginners.

Celtic Spirituality. After Patrick (c. 389–c.461) evangelized among the Celtic people, he established monasteries for men and women throughout Ireland. The abbots and abbesses (such as Brigid) of these monasteries provided spiritual oversight, and exposure to the writings of the desert fathers prompted strict ascetic practices. The "white martyrdom" of asceticism often included daily reciting of all 150 Psalms; the "blue martyrdom" spoke of exceptional penance for sin (e.g., lengthy praying in icy water); and the "red martyrdom" referred to the shedding of blood. The Celtic practice of private confession with specific penances later spread to the rest of the Western Church, and the Celtic concept of the *anamchara,* or "soul friend" influenced the Catholic practice of spiritual direction. The Celtic tradition is marked by beautiful prayers, such as the famous "St. Patrick's Breastplate."

SPIRITUALITY IN THE MEDIEVAL CHURCH

General Trends. The period from c. 600–c. 1500 was characterized by the spread and consolidation of the church throughout northern and eastern Europe, and during these centuries the Anglo-Saxon, German, Scandinavian, Ukrainian, and Russian cultures were "Christianized." The same period, however, also saw a declining Christian influence in Africa and Asia. In addition, the Latin West (centered in Rome) and the Greek East (centered in Constantinople) became increasingly alienated, and formally separated in 1054. In the West, the Dark Ages were followed by a period of high scholasticism in the Roman Catholic Church, and theological systemization was generally separated from mysticism. By contrast, the Eastern Orthodox Church never made such a distinction between theology and mysticism; in Orthodoxy, church dogma and personal experience of the divine mysteries were inextricably bound.

The Eastern Church. The Trinitarian emphasis of the seven ecumenical councils from 325 to 787, the traditions of the Greek theologians, and the geographical and cultural distance between the Western and Eastern Churches led to distinctive beliefs and practices in the Orthodox Church. Orthodox spirituality is largely characterized by apophatic theology, and this is evident in the writings of mystical theologians like John Climacus (c. 570–c. 649), Simeon the New Theologian (949–1022), and Gregory Palamas (1296–1359). In *The Ladder of Divine Ascent,* John Climacus, abbot of the monastery on Mount Sinai before becoming an anchorite (a total solitary), described the stages of the mystical ascent of the soul to God. Simeon and Gregory were proponents of *hesychasm,* which refers to the practice of stillness, silence, and mystical prayer. Gregory distinguished the *energies* of God which can be known by humans, and the *essence* of God which cannot be known. The vision of God, though imperfect in this life, is possible through a synergy between divine grace and human will.

All of these theologians stressed the grace-given discipline of unceasing prayer, or the "prayer of the heart." The most common form of this continual "Jesus Prayer" is "Lord Jesus Christ, have mercy on me," but there are several variations. The Jesus Prayer is also known as a breath prayer, since it is associated with breathing; it is designed to lead beyond thoughts to a state of *hesuchia,* or stillness, as it unites the mind and the heart. Another attribute of Orthodox spirituality since the Byzantine period of the church is the use of distinctively styled paintings as objects of veneration. These icons function as windows on eternity and are supposed to be used as vehicles through which one venerates the person represented in the image.

Monasticism. In the Western Church during the Middle Ages, the whole monastic system was reformed and expanded. A stable communal life was made possible through the spiritual disciplines of self-denial and voluntary submission that related to the three vows of poverty, chastity, and obedience. The early scholastic thinker Anselm of Canterbury (c. 1033–1109), best known for his contributions to systematic and philosophical theology, was also immersed in monastic life. Before he became the Archbishop of Canterbury, Anselm served as the abbot of the monastery of Bec in Normandy where he developed the poetry of intimate, personal devotion in his *Prayers and Meditations.*

The Carthusian Order was a strictly contemplative order of monks founded by Bruno (c. 1032–1101) in 1084. This stringent approach to monastic spirituality demanded perfect renunciation, mortification, silence, and solitude.

Bernard of Clairvaux (1090–1153) was a monastic reformer who administered a vast network of Cistercian monasteries throughout Western Europe. He has been called "Doctor Mellifluus" because of the sweetness of his teachings in contrast to the harshness and aridity of a number of medieval writers. His book on *The Love of God* distinguishes three stages of the spiritual life (animal, rational, and spiritual) and four degrees of love (loving self for one's own sake, loving God for one's own sake, loving God for God's sake, and loving self for God's sake). Like his contemporaries, he accepted the fourfold method of interpreting Scripture that was inherited from earlier writers like Origen and John Cassian: (1) literally (in the historical context), (2) allegorically (seeing Christ throughout Scripture), (3) tropologically or morally (obedience to moral instruction), and (4) anagogically (the contemplative level). Thus, his *Sermons on the Song of Songs* use the erotic language of the Song of Songs to develop the spiritual theme of the soul's personal intimacy with God.

Bernard's close friend William of Saint-Thierry (c. 1085–1148) was the abbot of the Benedictine abbey of Saint-Thierry before he resigned that post to become a Cistercian monk. Like Bernard, William wrote on the Song of Songs and portrayed it as the contemplative union between the soul and Christ. In *The Golden Epistle,* William eloquently combines intellectual illumination with ardent spiritual love as he outlines the journey of grace through which one finds, possesses, and enjoys God.

Mendicant Orders. The thirteenth century saw the development of a new approach to monasticism that embodied greater involvement and service in the world. Mendicants, or friars who lived by begging alms, were organized in religious houses under the direction of priors. Dominic Guzman (c. 1170–1221) founded an Order of Preachers known as Dominicans that was devoted to theological study and preaching. Until the fifteenth century, this order practiced individual and corporate poverty, and the Dominican stress on education produced great scholars like Albertus Magnus (c. 1200–1280) and his pupil, Thomas Aquinas (1225–1274), known as "Doctor Angelicus," who was the high-water mark of scholasticism. Works like the *Summa Theologica* and the *Summa Contra Gentiles* reveal Aquinas's genius for systematizing theological truths, but his writings were also infused with a living understanding of experiential spiritual knowledge. When he was urged near the end of his life to complete his *Summa,* he replied that everything he had written seemed like straw in comparison to what was revealed to him in his contemplation of God.

The Franciscan Order, another order of mendicants, was founded by Francis of Assisi (1181 or 1182–1226). Francis's joy, simplicity, love of nature, generosity, faith, and passion for Christ were infectious, and his associates (known as "Friars Minor," or little brothers) went on ever-widening missions in service of others. *The Little Flowers of St. Francis,* a collection of legends and traditions about Francis, gives a beautiful portrait of the vitality and spirit of the early Franciscans. Clare of Assisi (1194–1253) founded a Second Order for women known as the Poor Clares, and a Third Order known as the Tertiaries, or Brethren of Penitence, was founded for laypeople who sought a dedicated spirituality in the routines of ordinary life. Bonaventure (1221–1274), known as "Doctor Seraphicus," was the greatest of the Franciscan theologians. Bonaventure stressed that in comparison to the mystical illumination that God graciously grants to those who pursue Him, the most illustrious human wisdom is folly.

Other mendicant orders include the Carmelites (reorganized in the thirteenth century), the Augustinian Hermits or Friars, and the Capuchins (a later offshoot of the Franciscan Order that stressed poverty, austerity, and preaching).

Continental Mysticism. Highly mystical writings flourished both on the European continent and in England in the twelfth through the fifteenth centuries. These works must be read with careful discernment, since they are alloys that consist of varying proportions of gold and gravel. The gold is made up of authentic spiritual insights and powerful imagery, while the gravel may be composed of unbiblical teaching, psychological hysteria, or various degrees of pantheism.

Hugh of St. Victor (c. 1096–1141) was a mystical theologian who lived at the Augustinian monastery of St. Victor near Paris. Hugh's work was strongly influenced by the Platonic tradition, and he wrote a commentary on *The Celestial Hierarchy* of Pseudo-Dionysius. Another Victorine, Richard of St. Victor (d. 1173), was the first medieval mystic to systematically examine the psychology of mystical experience. He distinguishes the three ascending mental activities of thinking, meditation, and contemplation, and his works *Preparation of the Soul* and *Contemplation* progress from the contemplation of visible things to the contemplation of invisible things, and from there to the final transforming union.

Hildegard of Bingen (1098–1179) was the founder and first abbess of the Benedictine community at Bingen on the Rhine. This remarkable woman composed liturgical music and wrote books on natural science and medicine, the first known morality play *(Play of Virtues)*, and visionary literature. In her most important work, *Scivias*, she dictated an extensive account of 26 visions she received as a *summa* of Christian doctrine on such matters as the nature of the universe, the kingdom of God, the fall of man, sanctification, and the end of the world.

Amalric of Bena (d. c. 1207) was a pantheistic mystic who was a master at the University of Paris. He taught that when the soul rises to God by means of love, it loses its distinctiveness from God and becomes God Himself. Although his teaching was declared heretical, it influenced pseudo-mystical groups like the Brethren of the Free Spirit.

Mechthild of Magdeburg (c. 1210–c. 1280), like Hildegard of Bingen, was a German mystic and spiritual writer who experienced vivid pictorial visions. In *The Flowing Light of the Godhead,* Mechthild sometimes used the language of ecstasy and elevated eroticism to describe the divine presence. Her vision of the Sacred Heart contributed to later Roman Catholic devotion.

The German Dominican mystic Meister Eckhart (c. 1260–c. 1327) made significant but flawed contributions to mystical theology in his commentaries on Genesis and John, in his sermons, and in his treatises (e.g., *The Book of Divine Consolation*). Eckhart described himself as "God-intoxicated" and distinguished the *God* of religious experience who is revealed in the form of a Person, from the *Godhead,* which is an undifferentiated and unrevealable eternal Unity that transcends all human understanding. Because of his pantheistic tendencies, a number of his statements were condemned as heretical.

The teachings of Hildegard, Mechthild, and Eckhart strongly influenced a fourteenth-century spiritual and mystical movement

that came to be known as *Gottesfreunde,* the Friends of God.
Those in this company contrasted the externality of the ecclesiastical institutions with the inward and personal transformation
made possible by spiritual union with God. The anonymous
Theologia Germanica crystallized the spirituality of the Friends of
God movement, and this significant volume later influenced
Martin Luther. The *Theologia* taught that the differentiated temporal world must be transcended before the soul can know the
undifferentiated Divine Reality.

Johann Tauler (c. 1300–1361), a German Dominican, was an
inspirational preacher and teacher in the Friends of God movement. Tauler was strongly influenced by the mystical theology of
Meister Eckhart and taught three stages of self-dying: mortification in hope of heaven, spiritual and physical deprivations with no
thought of self, and complete harmonization with God's will. His
contemporary Henry Suso (Heinrich Seuse; c. 1295–1366) was
another Dominican associate of the Friends of God. His autobiographical *Life of the Blessed Henry Suso* describes his ecstatic
visions, and his *Book of Eternal Wisdom* bears the pantheistic overtones of his mentor Meister Eckhart. Suso's highly unstable spirituality was marked by ferocious mortification and self-inflicted
torments.

The Flemish mystic Jan van Ruysbroeck (John Ruusbroec;
1293–1381), a close friend of Tauler and Suso, was influenced by
the writings of Augustine, Pseudo-Dionysius, Bernard of
Clairvaux, and Meister Eckhart. His treatises *(The Spiritual
Espousals, The Sparkling Stone, A Mirror of Eternal Blessedness,* and
The Little Book of Clarification) made a profound impression on
his time by combining both the intellectual and the affective
strands of mysticism. Ruysbroeck insisted that the traditional
purgative, illuminative, and unitive stages are cumulative rather
than sequential. In *The Sparkling Stone,* he developed a progression from an active life (a good person who serves others), to an
interior life (a spiritual person who yearns for God and purges
creaturely images from the imagination), and finally to a contemplative life (a contemplative person who experiences loving union

with God but can remain active in the world). The third stage is attained only by a few, and then only momentarily.

Gerard Groote (1340–1384), a disciple of Ruysbroeck, was the founder of the Brethren of the Common Life (a lay association that had some connections with the Friends of God movement). The members lived in community and called this movement *Devotio Moderna,* the "Modern Devotion." Groote's preaching against the decadence of the church was empowered by his deep personal experience of the Holy Spirit.

Thomas à Kempis (c. 1380–1471), who wrote a biography of Gerard Groote, was the probable author of the enduring spiritual classic *The Imitation of Christ.* The spirituality of the Brethren of the Common Life was based on the life of Christ as the true center of the soul, but it overreacted to the abuses of scholasticism and devalued the intellectual life. This is reflected in *The Imitation of Christ* which also tends to negate the things of the created order.

Like Thomas à Kempis who was born the year she died, Catherine of Siena (c. 1347–1380) reacted to the corruption and degeneracy of the medieval church. Although she experienced visions, ecstasies, and demonic struggles, Catherine differed from many mystics by cultivating an altruistic spirituality that was engaged with social concerns. She practiced strict austerities, but her love for Christ compelled her to serve the sick and the poor.

Nicholas of Cusa (c. 1400–1464), a German cardinal and philosopher, was a gifted thinker whose mystical theology of spirituality *(On Learned Ignorance, Dialogue on the Hidden God, On Seeking God, On the Vision of God, On the Summit of Contemplation)* pointed beyond the boundaries of human reason. He argued that the road to truth leads to the *coincidentia oppositorum,* the "coincidence of opposites" in the Person of God (e.g., God is infinitely great and infinitely small, the center and the circumference, everywhere and nowhere, etc.).

Catherine of Genoa (1447–1510) combined rigorous personal discipline with active philanthropy (she established the first hospital in Genoa). After a decade of an unhappy marriage, she had a profound spiritual experience that transformed her life.

Catherine's mysticism was focused more on the infinite God than on the Person of Christ, and she felt submerged in the immensity of God's love.

English Mysticism. England in the later Middle Ages produced a number of prominent contemplatives who sought the grace of God to achieve unmediated knowledge of God through transcendent prayer. Richard Rolle (c. 1300–1349) studied at Oxford, later became a hermit, and wrote widely in English as well as Latin. His mystical life included periodic experiences of fiery warmth and the sweetness of heavenly music. His treatises (e.g., *Meditations on the Passion, Ego Dormio, The Form of Living*) center on a passionate devotion to Christ and encourage reading, prayer, and meditation.

The unknown author of the fourteenth-century devotional classic *The Cloud of Unknowing,* was familiar with Rolle's writings and was also inspired by Pseudo-Dionysius, Thomistic theology, and Rhineland mystics like Johann Tauler. *The Cloud of Unknowing* develops an apophatic mysticism of darkness that stresses the incomprehensibility of God and instructs the advanced reader in the proper ordering of the contemplative life.

Walter Hilton (d. 1396) was influenced by Richard Rolle and *The Cloud of Unknowing,* and in his principal work, *The Scale of Perfection,* he distinguished two stages of reform in faith and reform in feeling. For him, the highest degree of contemplation was a combination of cognition and affection.

Julian of Norwich (c. 1342–c. 1416) lived as an anchoress (a solitary), and in May 1373 she received sixteen visions or "showings." These *Revelations of Divine Love* are described in a shorter, earlier text and in a longer, later text. Her visions of the Passion of Christ and of the Holy Trinity led to a realization that divine love is the answer to all the mysteries of existence, including the problem of evil.

SPIRITUALITY IN THE MODERN CHURCH

The Protestant Reformation. There were a number of reformers like John Wycliffe (c. 1329–1384), the Lollards, John Huss (c. 1369–

1415), and William Tyndale (c. 1494–1536) who addressed the growing moral, doctrinal, and spiritual corruption of the church. But the actual Protestant withdrawal from Roman authority took place in four movements: the Lutheran and Reformed branches of Protestantism, the Anabaptists, and the Anglicans.

Lutheran Spirituality. After Martin Luther (1483–1546) realized that people are justified by grace alone through faith alone, he eliminated practices that sought to merit rather than receive the grace of God, such as prayers to the saints, indulgences, relics, pilgrimages, and vows of celibacy. He also introduced new elements to corporate spirituality, including the singing of hymns and the use of the vernacular Bible. Although he appreciated the mystical tradition in the *Theologia Germanica,* Luther was opposed to the apophatic mysticism inherited from Meister Eckhart and others. His was a more kataphatic spirituality of the cross that was based on biblical revelation and personal reception of the grace of God made available through the redemptive work of Christ.

Johann Arndt (1555–1621) was more concerned with communicating Luther's Christian experience than in codifying his theology. His sermons and writings like *True Christianity* promoted spiritual renewal and provided the groundwork for later Lutheran Pietism. By contrast, Jakob Boehme (1575–1624) was an unorthodox Lutheran mystic whose terminology had more in common with alchemy and astrology than with the Scriptures.

Reformed Spirituality. The Swiss reformer Ulrich Zwingli (1484–1531) was more radical than Luther in his rejection of Catholic tradition. Zwingli's spirituality of the Word minimized the liturgical, aesthetic, mystical, and sacramental aspects of corporate worship and eliminated any practices that were not commanded in the New Testament (e.g., vestments, visual art, and musical instruments in church).

John Calvin (1509–1564) took a more moderate position than Zwingli. After escaping from France to Switzerland, he directed the new religious and political order of Geneva. In his *Institutes of the Christian Religion,* Calvin stressed that every person who has been called by the sovereign grace of God into a faith relationship with Christ possesses a mystical "in Christ" union. Calvin understood this union to be a present possession resulting from the gift of sanctification that accompanies justification. This is very different from the usual medieval mystical approach to union with God as the product of a progressive series of spiritual or contemplative stages.

Anabaptist Spirituality. The Anabaptists, or "rebaptizers," generally affirmed "believers' baptism," and this led to the practice of rebaptizing those who had been baptized as infants. This was the most radical and unstable of the Reformation movements, and most Protestants as well as Catholics were vigorously opposed to these groups. Some held that direct inspiration from God superseded biblical doctrine, and this spiritual anarchy was paralleled by political anarchy. By contrast, Menno Simons (1496–1561), the founder of the Mennonites, gathered fragments of these groups into a more stable and less emotionally driven movement that encouraged its members to avoid immorality and false teaching. In general, Anabaptist spirituality is characterized by dependence on the inspiration of the Holy Spirit in worship, close community, simplicity in lifestyle, uncompromising morality, separation from worldly culture, and pacifism.

Anglican Spirituality. Thomas Cranmer (1489–1556) was the chief architect of the 1549 *Book of Common Prayer.* His stylistic genius enabled him to synthesize a liturgy that continues, in revised form, to be used throughout the world today. The collects, or common prayers in this book (Cranmer wrote some, but he derived most of them from the medieval Sarum Missal and Breviary), are among the most beautiful prayers in the English language.

Anglican spirituality has been immeasurably enriched by the metaphysical poetry of John Donne (1571 or 1572–1631), George Herbert (1593–1633), and Henry Vaughan (1622–1695). Donne's religious poems and sermons are marked by subtlety and striking imagery, and they are often centered in the Passion of Christ, human sinfulness and mortality, and the quest for salvation. Herbert's spiritual poetry, especially his collection of poems entitled *The Temple,* is redolent of an intensely personal relationship with God.

Other notable Anglican writers include Jeremy Taylor (1613–1667), author of *The Rule and Exercise of Holy Living* and *The Rule and Exercise of Holy Dying;* William Law (1686–1761), author of *A Serious Call to a Devout and Holy Life;* and the High Churchman and poet John Keble (1792–1866), author of *The Christian Year.*

The Catholic Reformation. The Catholic Counter-Reformation, centered in the Council of Trent (1545–1563), was a conservative response to the theological challenges of the Protestants and to the need for significant institutional reform.

Spanish Spirituality. Ignatius of Loyola (c. 1491–1556) founded a new religious order in 1540 called the Society of Jesus, or the Jesuits. This order became the spearhead of the Counter-Reformation and the fountainhead of missionary endeavors in America, Africa, and Asia (e.g., Francis Xavier). Loyola wrote a manual for spiritual direction in retreats called *Spiritual Exercises,* and this highly structured Ignatian approach to prayer and spirituality has continued to be used to the present time.

Teresa of Avila (1515–1582) was a reformer of the Carmelite Order and a perceptive interpreter of mystical experience and spiritual development. *The Way of Perfection,* her *Life,* and *The Interior Castle* develop the spirituality of prayer, meditation, and contemplation and describe the soul's journey to God through the purgative, illuminative, and unitive stages. The seven mansions in *The Interior Castle* are self-knowledge; detachment; humility and aridity; affective prayer; beginning union with God; mystical experience and the prayer of quiet; and peaceful union with God.

John of the Cross (1542–1591) was profoundly affected by Teresa, and his own spiritual development was forged in a life of pain, conflict, and passion for God. In *The Ascent of Mount Carmel* and *The Dark Night of the Soul* he described the purgation of the soul by the "night of the senses." After a period of rest, this night may be followed by a second painful purification, the "night of the spirit," in order to prepare the soul for the transforming union of spiritual marriage described in *The Living Flame of Love.*

French Spirituality. Francis de Sales (1567–1622) is best known for his *Introduction to the Devout Life,* a product of his spiritual direction of a number of individuals. In his writings, de Sales stressed that a life of holiness is not limited to the clergy or religious, but is also available to those who are active in the world. Salesian spirituality emphasizes a resolute volitional commitment to God regardless of emotional distractions.

Pierre de Bérulle (1575–1629), a friend of de Sales, founded a distinct school of French spirituality that detailed the cultivation of the interior life. Brother Lawrence of the Resurrection (Nicolas Herman; c. 1611–1691) wrote a devotional classic, *The Practice of the Presence of God,* that chronicled his practice of God's presence in the routines of daily activities. The philosopher and mathematician Blaise Pascal (1623–1662) had a transforming spiritual experience in 1654 that led to a spirituality of the heart (outlined in his extraordinary *Pensées*) that was centered on faith in the person of Christ as Savior. Pascal was influenced by Jansenism, a morally rigorous movement with predestinatory overtones that challenged Jesuit theology and practice and was denounced by the Catholic Church.

Another movement called Quietism was also denounced by the Church. A Spanish priest named Miguel de Molinos (c. 1640–1697) was condemned for his advocacy of the "holy indifference" of spiritual passivity and complete surrender of the will in his book *The Spiritual Guide.* Madame Jeanne-Marie Guyon (1648–1717) and her spiritual correspondent François Fénelon (1651–1715) were influenced by Molinos and were persecuted for popularizing the passive prayer of Quietism. Guyon's books, *Short and Very Easy Method of Prayer* and *The Spiritual Torrents,* taught that all distinct ideas, including the attributes of God and the mysteries of the life of Christ, should be avoided in mental prayer. Fénelon's *Spiritual Letters* and *Christian Perfection* provide practical guidance to the process of total abandonment of the self to God.

John Pierre de Caussade (1675–1751) sought to restore a balanced approach to mysticism in view of the overreaction to

Quietism, and his *Abandonment to Divine Providence* stressed the powerful theme of "the sacrament of the present moment."

Charles de Foucauld (1858–1916) and "The Little Flower" Thérèse of Lisieux (1873–1897) are two more recent examples of spiritual abandonment and the practice of renunciation in small things.

Protestant Movements. Following the Reformation period, the Lutheran and Reformed movements went through three developmental periods. In the confessional period, leaders attempted to define and defend their doctrinal positions. The Pietist period reacted to this preoccupation with dogmatic orthodoxy and called for a living faith and personal devotion. The rationalist period (which overlapped the Pietist period) reflected the Enlightenment view that autonomous human reason could arrive at final truths and could test revelatory claims. The influence of radical biblical criticism, evolutionary theory, and antisupernaturalism withered the spirituality of many mainline church leaders and often reduced religious practice to the teaching of universal ethical norms.

Puritans. The Puritans sought to purify the Anglican Church by bringing it into greater conformity with Reformed theology and practice. Puritan spirituality centered on self-examination and personal faith, and minimized "popish" trappings such as church ornamentation, vestments, and organs.

The well-known Puritan John Bunyan (1628–1688) suffered imprisonment because of his convictions, and he produced some of his writings in prison. After writing his autobiography, *Grace Abounding to the Chief of Sinners,* he wrote his enduring classic, *Pilgrim's Progress,* an allegory of the Christian life as a struggle between desires that are prompted by the world versus the upward call of God.

Quakers. The Society of Friends, founded by George Fox (1624–1691), renounced many of the practices of external religion and centered on a corporate mysticism which involved waiting for the Holy Spirit to speak through people in their meetings. The life and *Journal* of the American anti-slavery campaigner John

Woolman (1720–1772) illustrates the Quaker spirituality of sacrifice, simplicity, social justice, and humanitarianism.

Pietists. Philipp Jakob Spener (1635–1705) was the founder of German Pietism, a movement that called Lutherans out of their spiritual lethargy to a vital spirituality. His *Pia Desideria (Pious Hopes)* advocated such radical things for the time as lay activism, midweek Bible studies, sermons that edify rather than display erudition, and the teaching of pastoral care in seminaries. August Hermann Francke (1663–1727), a teacher who expounded the Bible along devotional lines, extended Pietist reform to a socially sensitive spirituality by founding orphanages, schools, and other institutions.

Pietism, with its emphasis on inward personal conversion and outward practical renewal, later spread to Scandinavian Europe where it challenged the conventionalism of the state churches. The negative side of this movement was its tendency toward legalism, self-righteousness, and anti-intellectualism.

In a class by himself, Sören Kierkegaard (1813–1855) attacked both Hegelian rationalism and the spiritual lethargy of the Danish church in his profound existential writings. In his *Either/Or* and *Stages on Life's Way,* he developed three stages or spheres of existence that he called aesthetic, ethical, and religious ("religion A" or "religion in the sphere of immanence," and "religion B" or "religion in the sphere of transcendence"). His spirituality of inward passion and subjective appropriation is developed in many of his books such as *The Sickness Unto Death, Fear and Trembling,* and *Christian Discourses.*

Evangelicals. The eighteenth-century Church of England saw a similar pietistic movement in response to the growing religious and moral torpor of the time. This spiritual deadness was caused in part by the influence of Enlightenment rationalism, and it was refreshing for many to hear the fervent preaching of evangelicals like John Newton (1725–1807). Evangelical spirituality (illustrated in the moving *Letters of John Newton*) encouraged lay involvement and family prayer and Bible reading. Newton influenced another evangelical, William Wilberforce (1759–1833), to serve God by staying in Parliament instead of taking Holy Orders. As a result, Wilberforce promoted social reform and was largely responsible for the abolition of the slave trade. His *Practical View of the Prevailing Religious System of Professed Christians* called believers to personal repentance and Christian responsibility.

Evangelicalism was also associated with growing philanthropy and concern for unreached peoples, and this led to the formation of organizations like the Church Mission Society, the British and Foreign Bible Society, and the Baptist Missionary Society, whose first missionary was William Carey (1761–1834). This missionary-minded spirituality was characterized by a global perspective, intercessory prayer, and a love and concern for unmet people.

Revivalism. The two Great Awakenings in eighteenth-century America brought a revival-oriented spirituality marked by conviction of sin, personal repentance, and what Jonathan Edwards (1703–58) described as *Religious Affections.* The tradition of revivalistic preachers like George Whitefield (1714–1770) was carried on in the nineteenth century by evangelists such as Charles G. Finney (1792–1875) and Dwight L. Moody (1837–1899). Revival spirituality not only stresses repentance and personal conversion, but also prayerful preparation and waiting for the sovereign and sudden movement of the Holy Spirit (e.g., the lay prayer revival of 1857–1858 and the Welsh revival of 1904–1905).

Methodists. John Wesley (1703–1791) and his brother Charles (1707–1788) were influenced by *The Imitation of Christ* and William Law. Their highly disciplined approach to the spiritual life led to the charge of "Method-ism," but it was only after an unsuccessful missionary experience in Georgia that Wesley experienced true conversion at a meeting of Moravians on Aldersgate Street in London. Wesley's spirituality of the warm heart and fervent preaching made him unwelcome in Anglican churches, but it was only after his death that Methodism became a separate denomination.

Holiness Groups. The early Methodist emphasis on personal holiness and the possibility of "entire sanctification," or Christian perfection, prepared the way for Wesleyan-inspired holiness movements and organizations like the Salvation Army, founded by William Booth (1829–1912). This approach to spirituality focuses on the need for a second work of the Holy Spirit after conversion to empower a life of holiness. The Keswick victorious life conventions in England and America also stress the need for "practical holiness," though this movement has more to do with exchanged life spirituality.

Pentecostals. In the 1906 Azusa Street revival in Los Angeles, William Seymour (1870–1922) related the "second blessing" of the holiness movements to the Acts 2 Pentecostal experience of the baptism in the Holy Spirit. Speaking in tongues was the manifestation of this baptism, and this highly experiential approach to spirituality rapidly spread through new denominations like the Assemblies of God and the Church of God. Pentecostalism is now the fastest growing segment of Christianity throughout the world, largely because this approach to spirituality appeals to the emotions and is highly accessible to the poor and the uneducated.

Recent Spiritual Figures. Evelyn Underhill (1875–1941) turned to the study of the mystics in her spiritual struggles, and her books (e.g., *Mysticism, The Life of the Spirit and the Life of To-day,* and *Worship*) have done much to expose her twentieth-century audience to the spiritual wealth of Christian mysticism and the value of spiritual direction.

Frank Laubach (1884–1970) was a modern Brother Lawrence in his practice of abiding in the presence of Christ while engaging in the circumstances of daily life. He described his experience of constant awareness of Christ in his *Letters by a Modern Mystic* and *The Game with Minutes.* Like Laubach, Thomas Kelly (1893–1941) believed that "There is a way of ordering our mental life on more than one level at once." In *A Testament of Devotion,* he argued that it is possible to maintain the deeper level of divine attendance through mental habits of inward orientation.

A. W. Tozer (1897–1963) was an evangelical mystic who possessed both a rich knowledge of the Scriptures and an extraordinary intimacy with God. He was almost alone among his conservative evangelical peers in his familiarity with the writings of earlier spiritual writers, including the Catholic mystics. Two of his works, *The Knowledge of the Holy* and *The Pursuit of God,* are already becoming spiritual classics because of the way they inflame their readers to follow hard after God.

C. S. Lewis (1898–1963), the most important Christian apologist of the twentieth century, displays a remarkably integrated spirituality of both the mind and the heart in books like *Mere Christianity, The Screwtape Letters,* and his autobiography, *Surprised by Joy.*

Dietrich Bonhoeffer (1906–1945) was martyred for his denunciation of Hitler, and in his important works, *The Cost of Discipleship, Life Together,* and *Letters and Papers from Prison,* he expounded a spirituality of Christian community and radical discipleship in a corporate context.

Thomas Merton (1915–1968), a Cistercian monk, has done more than any other person in the modern era to communicate the riches of contemplative spirituality. His captivating autobiography, *The Seven Storey Mountain,* and his many books on spiritual formation (e.g., *Contemplative Prayer* and *New Seeds of Contemplation)* have made the practice of contemplative prayer more appealing and accessible to a contemporary readership.

Martin Luther King Jr. (1929–1968) illustrated a spirituality of social justice in his leadership in the civil rights movement, and his writings *(Letter from a Birmingham Jail, Strength to Love)* show that his social activism was rooted in his Christian convictions.

Henri Nouwen (1932–1996) was a skillful and perceptive advocate of the incorporation of spirituality in daily life. His many books (e.g., *Making All Things New, The Genesee Diary, The Wounded Healer, The Way of the Heart,* and *In the Name of Jesus)* make a compelling case for a lifestyle of solitude, silence, and prayer.

Dallas Willard *(The Spirit of the Disciplines, In Search of Guidance, The Divine Conspiracy)* and Richard J. Foster *(Celebration of Discipline, Freedom of Simplicity, Money, Sex & Power, Prayer: Finding the Heart's True Home)* are two recent advocates of the profound benefits of disciplined spirituality.

Recent Developments. The Second Vatican Council in 1962–1965 (Vatican II) marked a significant difference in Catholic spirituality and in Catholic-Protestant relationships. Tridentine (the Council of Trent, 1545–1563) and Vatican I (1868–1870) Catholicism generally held that only Roman Catholics are true Christians, that the laity has less access to spiritual perfection than the religious (members of religious orders, such as the Benedictines, Cistercians, Dominicans, Franciscans, and Jesuits), and that spirituality consists of progression toward the mystical vision of God. These assumptions have been challenged since Vatican II, and Catholic spirituality has become more accessible to the laity.

The ecumenical movement (e.g., the World Council of Churches, 1948) has sought to engender a spirit of reconciliation and Christian unity, though it has been vulnerable to the problem of reducing the Christian message to a lowest common denominator. Still, there has been increased awareness of a need for a more cross-cultural spirituality in which one culture balances and informs another, as well as efforts to achieve an ecumenical spirituality of worship (e.g., the community of Taize in France in which both Catholics and Protestants worship together).

Catholics and Protestants have also participated in the charismatic movement that has developed since the 1960s and 1970s. Unlike classical Pentecostalism, the charismatic movement has reached people in mainline denominations, and the effect has generally been to move people from a liberal theological stance to a more evangelical and Spirit-led approach to the faith.

Twelve-step spirituality has also grown in recent decades, and this model, derived from the twelve steps of Alcoholics Anonymous, has been adapted by many churches. The "recovery" movement promotes a spiritually-oriented methodology for assisting people who have been enmeshed in addictive behaviors. Books like *The Twelve Steps for Christians* seek to relate these steps to biblical principles.

The growing cultural embeddedness of psychology has generated a variety of self-focused (e.g., self-help, self-fulfillment, self-esteem, and self-actualization) approaches to spirituality that are more anthropocentric than Christocentric. Interest has also swelled in spiritual techniques for inner healing as well as the interpretation of dreams, and while some of these approaches can be quite helpful, they are susceptible to misuse and unbiblical theology. With ever-greater frequency, the psychology of Carl Jung has been uncritically applied to a spiritualized version of the process of "individuation." These psychological influences on Christian spirituality have produced a "mixed bag" of new insights and profound dangers.

The recent "creation-centered" spirituality must be approached with even greater caution. The Jesuit theologian Pierre Teilhard de Chardin (1881–1955) had experiences of the numinous in nature and developed a cosmic panentheistic spirituality. In books like *The Phenomenon of Man* and *The Divine Milieu* he argued that the cosmos is evolving into "Point Omega," the Body of Christ. Along similar lines, the Dominican priest Matthew Fox (*Breakthrough: Meister Eckhart's Creation Spirituality in New Translation* and *The Coming of the Cosmic Christ*) has discarded the fall-redemption theme and replaced it with a divinizing creation spirituality. These writers illustrate the growing tendency to conflate aspects of Christian spirituality with "New Age" thinking, and this is also evident in the popular books of former Catholic monk Thomas Moore (e.g., *Care of the Soul; The Re-Enchantment of Everyday Life*).

Orthodoxy. The practice of spirituality in Eastern Orthodoxy has changed little since the medieval period (see "The Eastern Church" above). Two important developments in the modern period are a newer version of the *Philokalia* and the worldwide popularity of *The Way of a Pilgrim.* The original *Philokalia* ("the love of beauty," referring to love of God as the source of all things beautiful) was a small collection of spiritual writings selected by Basil of Caesarea (c. 330–379). These included passages from Origen of Alexandria as well as some of the desert fathers. In the eighteenth century, Macarius of Corinth (1731–1805) and Nicodemus of the Holy Mountain (1749–1809) edited a vast collection of texts from the fourth to the fifteenth century. They published this larger version of the *Philokalia* in 1782, and it has had a pronounced impact on modern Orthodoxy. The spirituality of this collection stresses the need for spiritual direction, vigilance, attentiveness, stillness, and the continual remembrance of God.

Although the "Jesus Prayer" was developed between the fifth and eighth centuries, it was only in the twentieth century that it has come to be used on a large scale by Orthodox lay people. This is largely due to a book by an anonymous pilgrim that first appeared in 1884. *The Way of a Pilgrim* is a compelling account of a Russian pilgrim's exposure to the *Philokalia* and his effort to learn the secret of praying without ceasing. *The Way of a Pilgrim* has popularized the use of "the prayer of the heart" throughout the world as a means of achieving a state of stillness and awareness of the Lord's presence.

Latin America, Africa, and Asia. The widespread social injustice in Latin America led to the development of a theology of liberation from oppression, and this "liberation theology" has been adopted by theologians around the world. In contrast to traditional Catholic spirituality, liberation spirituality appeals to laypeople and focuses on communal action rather than interior mysticism. In many hands, this theology has been reduced to social and economic revolution with a spiritual veneer, but writers like Gustavo Gutierrez *(We Drink from Our Own Wells: The Spiritual Journey of a People)* and Jon Sobrino *(Spirituality of Liberation: Toward Political Holiness)* have sought to develop a biblical and spiritual foundation for this movement. When this approach is embedded in a personal and communal relationship to God, it challenges the excessive emphasis on individualistic psychology that is characteristic of North American spirituality.

Liberation concepts have also been adapted to spirituality in the African setting, particularly to the issues of foreign manipulation, poverty, oppression, and apartheid (e.g., Bakole Wa Ilunga, *Paths of Liberation: A Third World Spirituality;* John de Gruchy, ed., *Cry Justice! Prayers, Meditations and Readings from South Africa).* There has been a growing effort to contextualize the Christian faith in such a way that it is more compatible with African culture without compromising the message of the gospel.

In recent years, Christianity has seen unprecedented growth in Asia, and its encounter with Asian cultures has led to distinctive approaches to spirituality. The books of Kosuke Koyama *(Waterbuffalo Theology, Three Mile an Hour God, Mount Fuji and Mount Sinai)* and of A. J. Appasamy *(The Gospel and India's Heritage)* illustrate the need for cultural adaptations in spiritual formation.

TWELVE RECURRING ISSUES AND EXTREMES

As I reflected on the spirituality of the ancient, medieval, and modern churches, it became evident that there was a recurrence of a number of themes and issues during these centuries. There were also several pendulum swings, sometimes from one extreme to another, that relate to these issues. These extremes are always unbiblical, and they force an either/or perspective on a number of areas that are better viewed as both/and.

1. Religious versus Laity

Most of the spiritual figures mentioned throughout history were unmarried members of monastic communities and/or religious orders. The Catholic and Orthodox Churches have tended to separate the "religious" (referring to members of religious orders) from the laity, and it has only been in recent years that these churches have questioned the assumption that the laity has less access to spiritual perfection than the religious. To a lesser degree, this clergy/laity distinction vis-à-vis spirituality has been practiced in Protestantism as well, and this has resulted in the unbiblical assumption that progression toward the heights of spirituality is something to be left to the "professionals."

The time has come for the church to affirm that spiritual growth is God's intention for every believer. Indeed, the majority of the godliest characters in the Bible, such as Abraham, David, Daniel, and Nehemiah, were laypeople, not priests. However, it would be prudent to avoid the opposite extreme, which is to see no value in the lifestyle of chastity, poverty, and obedience that is pursued by those in religious orders. While Paul affirmed the value of marriage, he also made it clear that those who remain in a single state for the Lord's sake enjoy the advantage of "undistracted devotion to the Lord" (1 Corinthians 7:32–35).

2. Human Responsibility versus Divine Sovereignty

The church has seen frequent pendulum swings from an emphasis on human responsibility that overlooks divine sovereignty, to such a stress on the sovereignty of God that the human side of the coin is eliminated. (The former is associated with the extremes of Arminianism, while the latter is associated with the extremes of Calvinism.) Some of the spiritual figures in church history have placed so much importance on human works in their theology and spirituality that they have overlooked the grace of God in salvation and spiritual growth. This tendency appears far more frequently than its opposite, since the human heart is more naturally inclined to a works orientation than to a grace orientation (this is evident in the non-Christian religions of the world). However, it is possible to stress the role of sovereign grace in spiritual growth in such a way that it underplays the value of works borne out of obedience.

3. Legalism versus License

This continuum is similar to the one just discussed, but it focuses more on the practical outworking of the spiritual life. Legalism is striving in the effort of the flesh to achieve a human standard of righteousness, and license (or libertinism) is an attitude that takes the grace of God for granted and minimizes the consequences of sin. In the history of spirituality, the former extreme surfaces more frequently, and it is associated with an overemphasis on rules and regulations. The effort to quantify and measure spirituality generally reduces it to conformity with human expectations and standards. However, there are instances of the opposite extreme, such as the medieval mystical sects known as the Brethren of the Free Spirit.

4. Corporate versus Personal

It is healthy to pursue a balance of both corporate spirituality and personal spirituality. In the modern West, an excessive individualism and interest in the psychology of the self has often separated believers from the spiritual benefits of life in community. But it is also possible to focus so much on the institutional side of the church that the personal and inward aspects of Christian living are overlooked. Many great figures in the history of spirituality have achieved a balance between mutual servanthood in corporate life and a personal quest for spiritual depth. The extremes of social action without personal spiritual consciousness and spiritual individualism without social relevance are both unbiblical. The former is the trap of liberal Christianity, and the latter is the snare of conservative Christianity.

5. Creation-Denying versus Creation-Affirming

Most approaches to Christian spirituality in the history of the church have tended to minimize the wonder, glory, and splendor of the created order. The creation-denying influence of Gnosticism and Neoplatonism profoundly shaped ancient and medieval spirituality, and this dualistic philosophy (nature and the body as evil and spirit as good) continues to emaciate many in the body of Christ. An incarnational theology that affirms the beauty and goodness of God's work in the created order is a needed corrective. In recent decades, however, there has been a growth in "creation-centered" spiritualities that are moving toward the opposite extreme of panentheism or full-blown pantheism.

6. Self-Denying versus Self-Affirming

Some of the figures discussed (e.g., Henry Suso) carried asceticism to a fine art and practiced gruesome forms of self-abnegation. This practice of physical mortification and rigorous asceticism often went far beyond the biblical associations of repentance with fasting and sackcloth and led to a morbid correlation between self-inflicted pain and spiritual progress. Scripture teaches that God uses trials and adversities in our lives to draw us closer to Him, but this is very different from the self-mortifying practices of many in the history of the church. More recently, the opposite extreme of self-affirmation, self-realization, and self-actualization has been taking hold, and increasing numbers of people are on the quest for a shallow feel-good, self-help spirituality. It is easy to miss the biblical balance of finding abundant life through growing surrender to the lordship of Christ. True self-denial comes through the renunciation of self-centered strategies and through a spiritual and moral paradigm shift from an egocentric to a theocentric universe.

7. *Technique Orientation versus Spontaneous Orientation*

Many have sought to reproduce the spiritual vitality of others through the development of knowledge, skills, and techniques. For example, a misguided approach to the *Spiritual Exercises* of Ignatius of Loyola can lead to a formula-driven methodology of prayer and meditation. The opposite of a skill-based spirituality is a totally spontaneous and free-form spirituality that eschews all disciplines and structures. A more biblical balance is a relational spirituality that combines both form (structure) and freedom (spontaneity) in the pursuit of spiritual maturity.

8. *Christocentric Contemplation versus Theocentric Contemplation*

Christocentric contemplation refers to the pursuit of union with the Triune God through contemplation on the person and work of Christ as revealed in the New Testament gospels and epistles. This Christ-centered approach is illustrated in the writings of Bernard of Clairvaux and Thomas à Kempis. By contrast, the way of theocentric contemplation involves the movement from contemplation of the reflection of God's attributes in the created order to direct contemplation of the heavenly Archetype. The danger of an exclusively Christocentric spirituality is the practical minimization of the soul's attention to the Father and the Holy Spirit. The danger of an exclusively theocentric spirituality that centers on the coinherence of the Creator and the created is the blurring of the distinction between God and the cosmos. Both Pseudo-Dionysius and Meister Eckhart had a problem in this area;

in their writings, pantheistic images of absorption were more ultimate than an I/Thou relationship.

9. Doing versus Being

The pendulum swing between the realization of spiritual identity through outward action versus inward reflection has not lost momentum over the centuries of church history. In our own time and culture, it is easier for most of us to relate to the former more than the latter, but there are other times and cultures that stress being over doing. From a biblical perspective, who we are in Christ should determine what we do, but both are crucial, since concrete doing should flow out of abstract being.

10. Active versus Passive

This spectrum is similar to the second and ninth spectra discussed above, but it is more concerned with the dynamics of actively seeking God versus passively responding to God's initiatives. The activist extreme overlooks the fact that God's grace is always previous to our reception. The passivist extreme minimizes the reality of human responsibility in the spiritual journey. The length of this continuum can be illustrated by the distance between the social activism of doing things for God and the spiritual passivity of the Quietist teaching of "holy indifference" to the will of God. A better balance is an ongoing series of choices (active) to allow Christ to love and serve people through us (passive).

11. Kataphatic versus Apophatic

The history of spirituality well illustrates both the *via positiva* and the *via negativa* concerning the knowledge of God. As we saw earlier, kataphatic spirituality affirms the positive knowledge of God through His general revelation in nature and His special revelation in the written and incarnate Word or *logos*. By contrast, apophatic spirituality insists that God is unknowable to the human mind and transcends all temporal attributes. Making a distinction between acquired contemplation and infused contemplation, the apophatic way argues that one cannot *acquire* knowledge of God, but that God can choose to *infuse* transcendent knowledge. Scripture provides a balance between these two extremes by affirming the richness of God's manifold revelation (e.g., Hebrews 1:1–3) while at the same time declaring that the truths of God are "spiritually appraised" by those who have "the mind of Christ" and are inaccessible to the natural man (1 Corinthians 2:14–16).

12. Objective Truth versus Subjective Experience

The turbulent history of doctrinal development and spiritual formation reveals yet another continuum. This spectrum ranges from a totally objective orientation in revealed truth to a totally subjective orientation in personal experience. Catholic scholasticism and Reformed confessionalism illustrate one side of the spectrum, and medieval mysticism illuminates the other side. When objective truth is carried to an extreme, it can wither into a word-based rationalism divested of personal engagement. When subjective experience is carried to an extreme, it can degenerate into unbridled emotionalism, self-delusion, and hysteria. Thus, there are churches that promote truth without love, and churches that promote love without truth. Clearly, both truth and love are needed for a full-orbed spiritual life, but the history of spirituality reveals something of a division of labor. *In very general terms,* Catholic and Orthodox mystics have a richer depth of spiritual understanding and experience than Protestants because this has been the focus of their attention. Protestants, on the other hand, have a more developed understanding of biblical, systematic, and dogmatic theology than Catholics and Orthodox because this has been the focus of their attention. The relative shallowness of both liberal and conservative Protestant spirituality has created a recent interest among a number of Protestants in mining the treasures of Catholic and Orthodox spirituality. If those who do this retain a biblically grounded theology that enables them to discern the spirit of truth and the spirit of error, they will be far richer for the experience.

THE LADDER OF PERFECTION

The three stages of the Ladder of Perfection *(Scala Perfectionis)* were originally presented in the writings of Pseudo-Dionysius (c. 500) and further developed by later mystics like Jan van Ruysbroeck (1293–1381) and Teresa of Avila (1515–1582). The three stages, or ways, are preceded by *awakening,* which refers to the soul's initial encounters with God. These experiences can be slow and incremental or sudden and intense, but they lead to a growing awareness of the sinfulness of the self and the holiness of God.

The first stage is the *purgative* way, and this involves a process of purifying the soul through renunciation, contrition, and confession of blatant sins and willful disobedience. This process becomes more subtle as sins of omission and unconscious sins are gradually brought to the surface and renounced before God. Purgation involves brokenness, gradual death to the tyrannous dominion of the ego, and sometimes wrenching transfers of trust from self-reliance to reliance on Christ alone for the soul's well-being. The purgative way is a painful but needful process of finding Christ's life by losing one's own life (increasing mortification) and thus moving from anxiety to trust.

The second stage is the *illuminative* way, which refers to a growing realization of the presence of God within as one is increasingly consecrated to God. In this stage, prayer is less an activity or an appendage and more a vital reality that flows out of one's being. Life takes on an aura of the mystery of God as one moves toward what Nicolas of Cusa called "learned ignorance," an increased awareness of how little we really know. The illuminative way is often characterized by growing love and other-centeredness as one expresses love for God through acts of love and service to others.

The third stage is the *unitive* way, also described as contemplation and abandonment to grace. This stage involves a growing experiential understanding of the mystery of "you in Me, and I in you" (John 14:20) and "it is no longer I who live, but Christ lives in me" (Galatians 2:20). In his insightful book *Spiritual Passages,*

Benedict J. Groeschel uses the writings of Teresa of Avila and John of the Cross to develop the general pattern of the unitive way (see his chart of the purgative, illuminative, and unitive ways which follows). The first phase of contemplation, or simple union with God, begins with the prayer of quietness in which one is yielded to God through purified desire and simplified will. This may be followed by what John of the Cross called "the dark night of the senses," a time of dryness and painful stripping away of the intellectual and emotional assurances of God's presence and care. The second phase of contemplation, or full union with God, involves detachment from self and an absolute certitude of the indwelling presence of God. This phase may be accompanied by an occasional experience of spiritual ecstasy that Teresa called wonder or "rapture." John of the Cross described a second night which he called "the dark night of the spirit" that God may use to purge the last vestiges of self-will. The highest level of the spiritual mountain described by the mystics is transforming union, or "spiritual marriage." This union of all desire and complete harmony with God involves a transmutation of personal identity in Christ and the realization of the oneness described in John 17:20–23.

This experiential mysticism of ascent with its quest for perfection and communion with God needs to be balanced by the biblical insights that are developed in Reformation theology. The believer in Christ has already received "every spiritual blessing in the heavenly places in Christ" (Ephesians 1:3), and the gift of spiritual union with God is realized in the mystery of "Christ in you, the hope of glory" (Colossians 1:27). By reviewing the twelfth issue discussed above, you will see that the Ladder of Perfection with its purgative, illuminative, and unitive ways focuses more on subjective experience than on objective (biblical) truth. The danger of this focus is the mistaken assumption that spiritual union with God does not exist until it is realized in experience. This assumption is incompatible with the many biblical truths about the believer's radically new identity in Jesus Christ (see chapters 8 and 9). Though the best writers avoid this, the Ladder of Perfection can also be misconstrued as a product of human struggle and merit

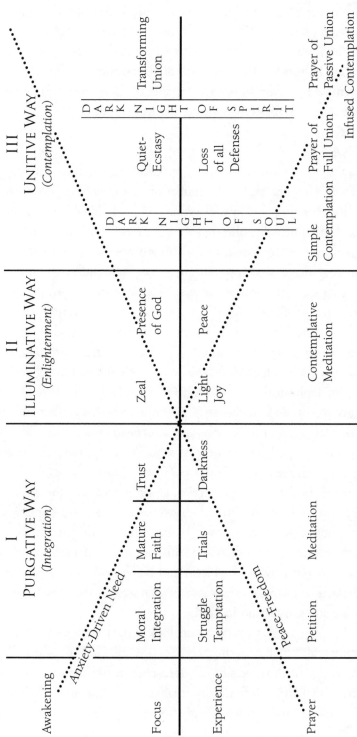

	I PURGATIVE WAY (Integration)			II ILLUMINATIVE WAY (Enlightenment)	III UNITIVE WAY (Contemplation)		
Focus	Moral Integration	Mature Faith	Trust	Zeal Presence of God		Quiet-Ecstasy	Transforming Union
Experience	Struggle Temptation	Trials	Darkness	Light Peace Joy		Loss of all Defenses	
Prayer	Petition	Meditation		Contemplative Meditation	Simple Contemplation	Prayer of Full Union	Prayer of Passive Union
							Infused Contemplation

Labels on the diagram: Awakening, Anxiety-Driven Need, Peace-Freedom.

Vertical text blocks: DARK NIGHT OF SOUL; DARK NIGHT OF SPIRIT.

From *Spiritual Passages: The Psychology of Spiritual Development* by Benedict J. Groeschel. The Crossroad Publishing Company. Used by permission.

more than the grace of God. From a biblical perspective, God's sovereign grace must infuse the whole process of spiritual formation in such a way that growth in sanctification is by grace through faith. The objective truth of our position in Christ is not determined by our subjective experience, but should gradually shape and be realized in our experiential practice.*

A VARIETY OF APPROACHES

The history of Christian spirituality reveals an enormous diversity of approaches and styles. A number of root metaphors dominate the insights and systems developed by individual writers and schools of spirituality through the centuries. In his helpful book *Thirsty for God,* Bradley P. Holt distinguishes six sets of these fundamental images that appear again and again in different contexts. The first set of metaphors depicts the basis of the Christian life as *rescue, redemption, and justification,* and these are central in the Lutheran and Reformed traditions (by contrast, Orthodoxy rarely uses the image of justification). The second set, *growth, unification, and healing,* focuses on the process of Christian living and is used metaphorically by Catholic mystics and experientially by Pentecostalists and charismatics. The third set depicts the spiritual life as *walking, journeying, climbing, and homing,* and these images of travel are used by a variety of schools and writers. The most popular example is John Bunyan's *Pilgrim's Progress.* The fourth set of images is *death and resurrection,* and this speaks of the cycle of departure and return, sin and forgiveness, despair and hope. The metaphor of progression toward resurrection in the life of God is characteristic of Orthodoxy. The fifth set of root metaphors is *battle and warfare,* and many Pietist and evangelical writers use these images. The sixth set, *thirst and hunger,* stresses the human need for life and satisfaction in God.

In appendix A, we took a brief look at the great variety of temperamental differences in people's psychological makeup and related this to the diversity of approaches to spirituality. You can also see that these differing spiritual styles are also strongly influenced by cultural factors. Clearly, someone raised in a context of eighteenth-century German Pietism would approach the spiritual life in a dramatically different way than if he or she were raised at the same time in France or in Russia.

The combination of your own nature (temperament) and nurture (culture) will predispose you to particular styles of spirituality, but as we argued before, it is helpful to stretch yourself through the discipline of deliberate exposure to a facet of spirituality you would ordinarily overlook or avoid. For instance, most of the readers of this book are probably unfamiliar with the practice of contemplative prayer. But in the history of spirituality, a surprising amount of emphasis has been placed on the importance of this form of prayer. Because of this, I recommend that you try developing skill in the practice of *lectio divina,* or sacred reading outlined at the end of Chapter 7.

Many writers through the centuries have distinguished three approaches to Christian living: the active life, the contemplative life, and the mixed life. The first focuses on doing more than being, the second focuses on being more than doing, and the third approach, which I recommend, is a balanced combination of being and doing in which the latter flows out of the former.

---

* My friend Bill Fagan describes six stages of spiritual growth that have some points of comparison with the purgative, illuminative, and unitive ways. The first stage is *spiritual birth*. This involves coming to an understanding of personal sinfulness and being justified in Christ (John 3, Romans 1–3). The second stage is *service*. Out of love and gratitude, the believer uses natural talents in an effort to serve God. Third, this leads to *frustrated inadequacy,* the painful Romans 7 discovery that we cannot live the spiritual life in our own power. The fourth stage is the experiential realization of our *identity with Christ* in His death, burial, and resurrection (Romans 6), and the awareness that Christ lives in us through the power of the Holy Spirit (Romans 8). The fifth stage is an ongoing process of reprogramming or *renewing of the mind* (Romans 12) that involves many cycles of surrender and trust, and of emptying and filling. The sixth stage is "graduation," or the *fullness of union with Christ* in the next life.

Kenneth Boa is engaged in a ministry of relational evangelism and discipleship, teaching, writing, and speaking. He holds a B.S. from Case Institute of Technology, a Th.M. from Dallas Theological Seminary, a Ph.D. from New York University, and a D.Phil. from the University of Oxford in England.

Dr. Boa is the President of Reflections Ministries, an organization that seeks to provide safe places for people to consider the claims of Christ and to help them mature and bear fruit in their relationship with Him. He is also president of Trinity House Publishers, a publishing company that is dedicated to the creation of tools that will help people manifest eternal values in a temporal arena by drawing them to intimacy with God and a better understanding of the culture in which they live.

Publications by Dr. Boa include *Cults, World Religions, and the Occult; I'm Glad You Asked; Talk Thru the Bible; Visual Survey of the Bible; Drawing Near; Unraveling the Big Questions about God; Night Light; Handbook to Prayer; Handbook to Renewal; Simple Prayers; Face to Face* (two volumes); *An Unchanging Faith in a Changing World;* and *That I May Know God.* He is a contributing editor to *The Open Bible*, the *Promise Keeper's Men's Study Bible, The Leadership Bible*, and the sole contributor to the *Two-Year Daily Reading & Prayer Bible.*

Kenneth Boa also writes a free monthly teaching letter called *Reflections.* If you would like to be on the mailing list, call:

(800-372-9632)
800 DRAW NEAR